The Art of Coarse Cookery

The Art of Coarse Cookery

SPIKE HUGHES

ILLUSTRATED BY DEREK ALDER

Well, at least a peck of dirt tastes of something

ANON

HUTCHINSON OF LONDON

HUTCHINSON & CO *(Publishers)* LTD
3 Fitzroy Square, London W1

London Melbourne Sydney Auckland
Wellington Johannesburg Cape Town
and agencies throughout the world

First published 1971

*This book has been set in Baskerville type, printed in Great Britain
on antique wove paper by Anchor Press, and
bound by Wm. Brendon, both of Tiptree, Essex*

ISBN 0 09 107410 X

'Tis an ill cook that cannot lick his own fingers
SHAKESPEARE

Contents

1	First Principles	7
2	Organisation	17
3	Technique	30
4	Ethics and Customs	99
5	Last Course	109
	Bibliography	111
	Conversion Tables	112

I

First Principles

Kissing don't last; cookery do!
GEORGE MEREDITH

'Cookery and the Artificial Preparation of Food,' said Mrs Beeton, helping her husband to another plateful of Omnibus Pudding (3 oz flour, 3 oz suet, 3 oz stoned raisins, 2 oz golden syrup, ¼ pint milk), 'has one chief object: to assist the wonderful series of changes known as digestion and assimilation.' A secondary aim, she went on, was 'to render certain foods, noxious in their natural state, fit for human consumption. The potato and manioc are poisonous when gathered, but rendered harmless by the cook.'

Admirable sentiments, full of nourishing commonsense, but, it must be said at once, entirely contrary to all the known principles of the Art of Coarse Cookery. For a start, Mrs Beeton has got what would nowadays be called her priorities wrong. Nobody for whom this study is intended would ever regard the chief object of cooking to be to 'assist in the wonderful series of changes known as digestion and assimilation'. To us there is nothing 'wonderful' about digestion or assimilation. You can either digest and assimilate or you can't, and you live your life accordingly.

The chief object of cooking anything, whether in a Boy Scout's billy-can or according to the tenets of the haughtiest *haute cuisine*, is to produce something good to

'. . . solely for his own amusement.'

eat. The Art of Coarse Cookery, however, differs from all other classes of cookery in one respect. While there are those who live to eat, others who eat to live, cooks who cook to live, and cooks who live to cook, the Art of Coarse Cookery is uniquely for those who cook to eat.

It may sometimes happen that the cooking turns out to be more enjoyable than the eating, but that is just one of the expected hazards of a strictly amateur pursuit in which the luck of the draw plays as characteristically important a part as it does in any other sporting event.

At this point, I think, the essentially amateur nature of Coarse Cookery should be emphasised. By 'amateur' I do not mean only those who do not cook for money or money's worth, but those who are amateurs in the best sense of the word. The Italians have an even better word, too often used in a contemptuously derogatory sense by the English, and that is *dilettante*: one who takes *diletto*, or delight, in the cultivation of a learned subject or the fine arts solely for his own amusement.

The fact that Coarse Cookery is primarily a pastime for the true *dilettante* naturally does not exclude many other categories of cook from joining in. They, too, can learn and benefit from close study of this manual, for there is no *cuisine* so *haute* that it cannot pick up a useful tip or two from Coarse Cookery. Even the overworked housewife, condemned to cook whether she likes it or not, will find something to console and encourage her in these pages.

Whether the Coarse Cook is born, or stimulated by environment, it is difficult to say; probably a little of both. But in every case the first manifestation of interest in cooking to eat is spontaneous. And in every case, of course, this manifestation takes a highly individual form.

When I was four years old I made friends with a village baker. I don't think I actually went so far as to want to be a baker when I grew up, but after constantly watching him knead the dough and finally roll it in flour and put it in the oven, I was fascinated enough by the ritual and the process and the unforgettable smell of new warm bread to want to try to make it myself.

I went home and learned from my mother that dough was made with flour and water; or so she thought. I mixed the flour and water to the right consistency, pushed it about a little, rolled it in flour and put it in the oven to turn into a cottage loaf. Since the British started boiling, instead of baking, their bread, it is possible you've never seen one; but you may learn from the dictionary that it consists of 'two round masses, smaller on top of larger'.

And that is just how my cottage loaf came out. For reasons which I found puzzling at the time, the loaf was not only uneatable: it was unbreakable. The two round masses were as solid (and if thrown, probably as lethal) as cannon balls. It was a disappointing result, but there was no doubt that it qualified as an essay in the Art of Coarse Cookery: I was cooking to eat, and if the cooking turned out to be more fun than the eating, then that was Coarse Cookery all over.

I went to the baker and told him what had happened. He explained to me that *his* bread was leavened and what I had made was unleavened—the most primitive form of bread known to man, and perhaps the first cooked food the human race had ever prepared. In later years it was a source of great self-satisfaction to realise that one had in fact started a lifetime of Coarse Cookery at the very beginning, with the most basic, elemental, primeval process of all.

Where one's first solo experiment in Coarse Cookery is usually highly individual, the next stage is one that must be common in this country to hundreds of thousands who were Boy Scouts when they were small boys, or Brownies when they were little girls. Speaking for myself, the first thing that appealed to me about the idea of being a Boy Scout was the prospect of being allowed—even encouraged—to cook as part of a test to be passed to raise me from the level of a tenderfoot to whatever the next rank was called. Learning to tie knots called sheep-shanks, clove hitches, running bowlines, fisherman's bends, running eyesplices, blackwall hitches and double sheet bends, though fascinating, was not of much practical use unless one had a boat to tie them on; but cooking was its own immediate reward and greatly relished by all.

The ingredients, in my experience, were limited. Neither I nor any former Scout or Brownie can remember ever having been given anything to cook but sausages. With an outdoor wood fire that had to be lit by using no more than three matches (this was a condition of passing the test), and the only cooking utensils a billy-can and a fork, the *repertoire de cuisine* affecting sausages was extremely limited. Baking was out, and so was grilling unless you had brought a toasting fork with you. The only possible way was to put the sausages in the billy-can and let them stew in their own juice.

As with all classes of cookery, in this primitive form of Coarse Cookery the preparation was important, and sometimes almost interminable. The worst thing was the business about having to light the fire with three matches. When he set out the condition of this cooking test one can only suppose that the late Lord Baden-Powell must either have done all his sausage-cooking on an absolutely windless day, or lit his fire with those sulphuric wind-proof matches the French call *allumettes chimiques*.

The underprivileged tenderfoot, however, never by any chance had a windless day for his cooking, nor did he have access to those lucifers. On the other hand, failure to light the fire with three safety matches which blew out as soon as you struck them, did not deter one from using up half a box of matches in order to get the fire going somehow and so achieve one's principal object—cooking sausages.

If you didn't pass the test because you'd used more than three matches that was no reason to go hungry; in fact, the longer you took over this particular test, the better. If you passed it too soon they'd put you on to something else, like putting trek carts together.

This youthful cooking of sausages, braised in a billy-can or roasted on a toasting fork, is, of course, a very primitive form of Coarse Cookery. It is none the less

'. . . having to light with three matches.'

genuine Coarse Cookery, performed with enthusiasm and pleasure with its aim the provision of something good to eat—at least, good according to the taste of the cook, where the cook is a small boy.

Nothing could be a greater mistake, however, than to regard all Coarse Cookery as primitive. As in all the arts, skill is developed with practice and experience, and so far from being primitive and elementary, Coarse Cooking can be surprisingly sophisticated. This is largely because the dedicated Coarse Cook does not hesitate to step in where other fools fear to tread.

I know of one such cook. His first steps in Coarse Cookery were taken in his teens with the successful preparation of a Wiener Schnitzel. He had been a student in Vienna and had learnt the recipe there. It was the only recipe he ever learnt and he has been cooking Wiener Schnitzels ever since—expense and availability of ingredients permitting.

Today he is a grandfather and still produces a delicious Schnitzel, though, as always, leaving his wife to cook the vegetables that go with it. Nobody in Vienna ever gave him a recipe for boiling potatoes, it seems.

This case is certainly unusual, but the specialist is not uncommon even in *haute cuisine*. There are cooks who spend a lifetime in the kitchens of great restaurants all over the world doing nothing but making sauces, or ices, or—for all one knows—Wiener Schnitzels.

Among the most important principles of Coarse Cookery that must be accepted is one admirably stated in 1846 by Charles Elmé Francatelli, 'pupil of the celebrated Carême, and Maître d'Hôtel and Chief Cook to Her Majesty the Queen'. In his view cooking was 'an art by which refined taste is to be *gratified* rather than a coarse appetite *satisfied*'.

The very mention of such a thing as a Coarse Appetite will shock and surprise the student of Coarse Cookery. It is something we never knew existed, and if it did exist, would never recognise or accept, since it is completely contrary to all the traditions and philosophy of our Art.

That we should take note of words spoken by Charles Elmé Francatelli is natural. We respect the past of cookery and learn from its history; and we revere the great figures whose invention and imagination continue to inspire us, and whose occasional eccentricities are often endearing. Who cannot take delight in M. Francatelli's immortal reference to 'the mirth-inspiring powers of Burgundy'? Or his emphatic classification of Burgundy as 'exciting', Champagne as 'captious', Roussillon as 'restorative' and Bordeaux as 'stomachic'? 'Captious', defined in the dictionary as 'fallacious', 'sophistical', 'fond of taking exception, trying to catch people in their words', seems a very quaint adjective indeed for Champagne; but then, equally, M. Francatelli's inclusion of the strong red wine of Roussillon is a little puzzling since his only reason for including it is to recommend it to those 'who are a prey to spleen—lowness of spirits—melancholy', as a 'pleasant remedy for their frightful ailments'. Which is no way for a Queen's maître d'hôtel to talk about wine.

It is a common illusion among the untutored that the Art of Coarse Cookery is not only primitive but un-disciplined, having neither rules nor regulations, and certainly not affected by the fundamental and universal truths of cookery set down in the classic writings of the Masters. Nothing could be further from the truth.

The true Coarse Cook is proud of his heritage, well-versed in its literature, and jealous of the good names of the Prophets who created it, but rarely, I think, touchy or easily provoked by the ignorance of the Philistine.

There are limits, of course, and there was understandable indignation when, some years ago, a London evening paper headed an item in its Stop Press: 'Fire in Haymarket Cafe.' The 'Cafe' (not café) proved, on reading further, to have been nowhere less than the Carlton Grill Room in the Carlton Hotel. To describe as a 'cafe' the scene of the immortal Escoffier's greatest gastronomic triumphs was too painful a reminder of the waywardness of modern Fleet Street. Kayff indeed!

The classics of cookery literature are what is called 'required' reading. But unlike most classics they are not read and put away out of sight. They become permanent stove-side books, constantly referred to, and quoted from, to settle the sort of disputes that arise whenever two or more Coarse Cooks are gathered together. The words of Francatelli, Curnonsky and Mrs Beeton, of Dolby and Carême, of Escoffier, Ude, of Trimalchio and Artusi encourage, inspire and comfort. Particularly Artusi.

Pellegrino Artusi was the author of a classic Italian volume called *The Art of Eating Well*, first published in the 1890s and now well beyond its 80th impression. He wore white whiskers twice as long as the Emperor Franz Josef's and began his book with the magnificent words: 'There are two principal functions in life: food and the propagation of the species.'

The order in which these functions are listed will not pass unnoticed by those whose hobbies have always been, in order of preference, wine, women and song.

The author was a Tuscan with outspoken views on food who never hesitated to say if he considered a dish revolting, but respected your right to freedom of choice by giving you the recipe in case you should ever sink so low as to want to use it. He considered that those dumplings known as *quenelles* could only have been invented by a chef whose master had no teeth.

The essential elements of what might be called the Deportment of the true Coarse Cook are something we can learn from the example of Pellegrino Artusi—humility, for instance, and modesty, and a fierce aversion to *chi-chi*. We naturally lack the authority which enables him to rebuke Brillat-Savarin for exaggerating the importance of *fondue*; but, like Artusi, we instinctively reject the overblown pronouncements of the ancient gastronomers whose language was every bit as extravagant as that of the wine jargonauts of today.

There was Athenaeus, for a start. He was a Greek grammarian born in Egypt, who around A.D. 230 affirmed that 'cooks were the first kings of the earth'. Then, a little later, we had Robert Burton (1577–1640) who proclaimed 'Cookery is become an art, a noble science, cooks are gentlemen'.

If we are naturally embarrassed by high-flown cookery talk we are certainly no more inclined to take the cooking life seriously. Not, I mean, to the extent which caused the famous Vatel, according to that old gossip Mme de Sévigné, to kill himself with his sword because at a banquet he had prepared in honour of Louis XIV in 1671, he saw to his horror that the fish course had not arrived. 'Knowing that he could not survive the disgrace of a dinner without fish, he stabbed himself with his sword and drew his last breath just as the fish arrived.'

I don't know about other classes of cook, but with us the non-arrival and, indeed, non-existence of dishes at the awaited moment is such a common occurrence as to be hardly worth mentioning, let alone committing suicide over.

Later commentators on the Vatel case have pointed out that he was not a cook: he was maître d'hôtel to the Prince de Condé. No cook, they say, would ever have given up as easily as that; he would have used his brains and made the best of a bad job.

It is a flattering thought that the Coarse Cook and the high-class category of *chefs de cuisine* these commentators had in mind should have in common the same instinctive reaction to unforeseen disaster in the kitchen. But judging by some of the restaurant meals we have eaten in our time there are quite a number of cooks around who would serve humanity better if they followed the example of Vatel and took the honourable way out.

But we are being uncharitable, and that is not really in our nature.

2

Organisation

Beauty from order springs
Art of Cookery, by WILLIAM KING (1663–1712)

Whatever else they did in their spare time, there is no doubt that the famous chefs and gastronomes of the past rarely missed an opportunity of making a statement. Asked by a reporter what he thought of recent technological breakthroughs in cookery, Louis Eustache Ude replied enigmatically: 'Music, dancing, painting, fencing and mechanics possess professors under twenty years of age, but pre-eminence in cooking is never attained under thirty.'

M. Ude, cook in turn to Louis XVI, the Duke of York, Crockford's and Lord Sefton (whose employ he left in disgust when he discovered one of his Lordship's guests adding pepper to his soup), was speaking of his own professional class, of course. Anybody who did not achieve pre-eminence in the Art of Coarse Cookery by the time they were thirty would have died of starvation—and shame—long before. Similarly, the Organisation of Coarse Cookery is something that cannot be embarked upon too soon in life.

The only form of Coarse Cookery that needs no organisation is in fact what is often the earliest—namely, the elementary Boy Scout sausage fry, when materials, equipment, and occasion are organised by somebody else. After that you're out on your own, relying unceasingly

'The seven stages of Coarse Cookery. . . .'

on your well-known national genius for improvisation, compromise and muddling through. (In passing, it is interesting that in French, German and Italian there is no equivalent word for 'coarse' as the English apply it to fishing, rugby, cricket, gardening, sailing and other spiritual pursuits. What a lot Europe missed by not joining the British Empire when there was one.)

The problems of the Organisation of Coarse Cookery have much in common with those of other coarse pastimes: the selection of time and place, the arrangement of fixtures, the choice of tolerant and enthusiastic companions with whom—or rather, on whom—to practise and experiment and so finally perfect the most chancy of all the domestic arts and sciences.

While human company and sympathy can be a help to morale, in Coarse Cookery one is concerned first and foremost with the organisation of the raw material and of the mechanical means of converting the inedible into the edible (without risk of *vice versa*).

As man passes through the seven stages of Coarse Cookery so these raw materials become more numerous and mechanical aids more complex and indispensable. The mewling infant Boy Scout we have seen needs nothing more than a billy-can, a couple of sausages and an endless supply of matches for his solitary *fête champêtre*.

The schoolboy, unwillingly at boarding school, needs (or gets) little more—a gas fire, a mug of coke, a loaf of bread (no Thou's at boarding schools—not in my day, unfortunately), and he is equipped to produce toast or crumpets. This is about the limit of his repertoire until he moves to the gas-ring cookery age.

It is at this period in a man's life that he makes his first definite step forward in the Art of Coarse Cookery. To all who live in digs—the student, the undergraduate, the young man about to qualify in his profession, the penniless but rarely starving artist—to all of these, and many like them, the gas ring opens a new world of adventure and richness.

For many people the bed-sitter gas ring provides them

with their first experience of the frying pan, and as everybody knows, the frying pan is at the root of all bad English cookery. Indeed, if there is a national motto it is 'When in doubt, fry it'.

But there is frying and frying, and the true Coarse Cook quickly learns how to use his new-found implement properly, though not before his keen-nosed landlady has hinted that burnt midnight oil shouldn't really smell quite like *that*.

With the possession of a frying pan the culinary repertoire is automatically extended—or shall we say that part of the repertoire that is based on fat and protein is extended. The cooking of vegetables to be eaten as an accompaniment to the main dish, if not impossible, is limited virtually to what you can get into the frying pan at the same time as the chop or steak—tomatoes, mush-rooms, onions. Otherwise, you have to wait until the solitary ring is vacant before you can start cooking anything in a saucepan to eat as a separate course.

Potatoes are not really recommended for bed-sitter gas-ring use; they have to be peeled, and few digs have facilities for that class of *haute cuisine*. The best use a saucepan can be put to at this stage is to heat a tin of soup; or to make coffee, in itself an important step in the artistic development of the Coarse Cook.

From the single gas ring the bachelor usually graduates to the flat with a kitchen (unless he takes the coward's way out and lives in a service flat). It is here that he begins to cook in earnest, where the profusion of gas flames, of hot plates, ovens, grills, regulos and thermostats produces flames and smoke and smells of a far more spectacular nature than anything he has encountered before.

It is at this stage, too, that he first begins to consult his friends, or perhaps even a book, about some of the more advanced processes of cookery—at least, they are advanced processes in Coarse Cookery. In other circles, such subtle touches as making tea with boiling water, or adding salt to the water you boil potatoes in, are considered very elementary. But to the Coarse Cook, entering Phase IV of his career, many processes others would regard as commonplace are still mysterious, and may even remain so for the rest of his life, if he does not accept advice when offered or asked for.

The next phase, the fourth of his seven ages as a cook, is when the bachelor begins to feed himself at home more often; he 'dines' out less frequently at the local off whatever they can offer in the way of sausages and mash, or cold pork pie and vinegary beetroot and bottle-dressed potato salad.

It is also the first time in his life he realises that not only is there more to shopping than just going out and buying things, but that the whole business is a mass of unimaginable fraughtfulness. It is fraught with disillusions, with frustration, and with disappointment. Rays of hope and hints of encouragement come only after bitter experience and the passing of endless time to unfraught it of its depressing load.

First, there is the butcher.

Ever since meat rationing was introduced in half the countries of Europe during the 1914 war, butchers have everywhere succeeded in playing hard-to-get. In times of peace and world-wide glut they still sell you meat as though they were doing you a favour.

Not all butchers deserve this reputation, of course, but it does not fade easily.

It is the butcher who confronts the fourth-stage Coarse Cook with the first unpleasant fact of shopping life that when you buy meat in England one-third of what you pay for you don't want to eat. Joints, steaks, chops, cutlets are all cut from animals specially bred, it seems, to be worth half their weight in fat. Any complaint is met with the boast that British meat, like the British Post Office, is the best and cheapest in the world. All objections that though meat may be more expensive in France, at least you can eat what you pay for, are swept aside as so much Communist propaganda.

I was going to say the butcher who shows no prices is not to be trusted. But one of the nicest butchers I know never marks his meat at all. This is because he likes to cut his profits and charge his really hard-up customers less than he charges the others, and he likes to do it discreetly.

If you *have* to deal with the wrong sort of butcher when you are young, then it is best to ask your daily, or the porter's wife, to buy your meat for you. Plead ignorance, lack of time; play the simple motherless bachelor. The butcher won't charge them half as much as he'd charge you, and the only people who know this are you and the butcher. And he doesn't know you know.

Shopping also brings the inexperienced Coarse Cook into contact with greengrocers. They are even more difficult than butchers. There are not only so many of them, but there are two distinct species—those with shops, and those with barrows or market stalls.

Of the two species the more infuriating is the first. You expect to have to be vigilant in the matter of the weights, measures and quality of the goods you buy from a barrow. It is part of the game. But static and mobile greengrocers are unmistakably brothers under the skin, and those with shops have to be watched too, because by having a shop they at once appear more respectable, and so give customers a confidence which can often be misplaced.

Shop or barrow, the only difference between them is that you pay more to be gypped indoors and out of the rain than outdoors and not.

Once again it is a question of paying for a lot of food you can't eat—for the mud on the potatoes, the tough outside leaves of cabbage, the inedible tops of leeks, the turnips riddled with maggots. All objections that though vegetables may be more expensive in France, they are presented attractively, look clean, and at least you can eat all you pay for, are swept aside as so much bourgeois propaganda.

It is quite possible that some who read this manual may consider the discussion of greengrocers and fresh vegetables superfluous. Why bother with them when frozen vegetables

'Performing before an audience.'

can be bought in the supermarket without argument or the need to examine them for faults and blemishes?

The truth is that the fundamental rule of all the Coarse Arts is that one should get the most for the least, and whatever it may say on the frozen packet, you get more good French beans for less money when they are fresh than when they are frozen. More than that: if you make a habit of buying frozen vegetables you will lose your proud status at once. You are cooking as though you were an average English restaurant. And whoever would want to take a girl to an average English restaurant for their first meal together when he has reached the fifth stage of Coarse Cooking?

All that has been said about shopping and the organisation of raw materials in this chapter has been to prepare the student for his first serious trial as a cook: the moment when he entertains a girl friend for the first time to a meal he has prepared himself. This is the fifth age of Coarse

Cookery, corresponding roughly to Shakespeare's third of the seven ages of man—the lover sighing like a furnace with a 'woful' ballad made to his mistress's eyebrow.

In our more materialistic age the fifth-stage Coarse Cook does not sigh like a furnace so much as sigh for an oven that will turn itself off when you want it to, and the skill to avoid a 'woful' salad that will raise his mistress's eyebrow in quite the wrong way. The technical problems of preparing this first tête-à-tête meal are in fact no different from any of those discussed later in the chapter on Technique; they only seem so for reasons of nervousness caused by the occasion and the lack of experience in performing before an audience. (As a consolation: if you have economic worries over the price of meat, the anonymous French author of the classic *Clarisse* reassures us that 'women do not eat too heartily of coarse meat dishes'.)

The five ages of Coarse Cooking Man so far discussed also apply to Coarse Cooking Woman. As a Brownie she may have cooked rock cakes instead of sausages, as a schoolgirl cocoa and hot buttered toast; her gas-ring cookery may have had a slightly more extensive repertoire than her male contemporary's, and she is more likely to have shared a kitchen with a flat full of co-tenants and so have cooked for room mates as often as for herself alone.

Her plan for entertaining her young man for the first time with a meal she has cooked herself may be more ambitious and varied than his for her, but she will suffer from the same anxieties and nervous apprehension—even though she has instinctively developed greater technical facility in adolescence by being a girl, and therefore likely to have come into close everyday contact with the kitchen.

But has she, in fact? It was not uncommon during the Second World War to encounter women who, deprived of all domestic help for the first time in their lives, found themselves entirely incapable of dealing with the elementary physics of cookery. My wife remembers how, early in the war, she was woken by an appalling smell coming from the kitchen. It was found to be caused by her mother boiling herself an egg. The saucepan had not boiled dry; there had never been any water in it. Nobody had ever said anything about water.

And if you think that story couldn't be repeated today, that the protected life enjoyed by my mother-in-law when young belongs to history, you would be surprised how many young brides come back from their honeymoons these days to be sent off smartly by their husbands to take a crash course in cookery.

The emergency cookery course does not often lead to a girl becoming a Cordon Bleu cook, but it is a prolific breeding ground of really first-class Coarse Cooks. It provides opportunity to pick up that little learning which is far from being a dangerous thing: it is all one wants.

More learning can lead to ideas above one's station— and that, in all the Coarse Arts, is the start of heresy that leads to social ostracism and a lonely old age.

Overheard Cordon Bleu shop talk can be invaluable as an aid to the formation of the store-cupboard—one of the most indispensable features of the sixth age of Coarse Cookery. For the sixth age is the age of the Kitchen Matrimonial, when mistakes made in kitchen-organisation can be rectified by resort to the store-cupboard.

Its use as a glorified culinary first-aid box is, of course, a secondary function of the store-cupboard. Its prime purpose is to serve as a reservoir of essential materials which the cook has to use before he can make the mistakes that oblige him to return to it in a hurry for help. Some of its contents, however, would never be used by any self-respecting cook except in an emergency. Tins of 'creamed' rice pudding, for instance, are something for the emergency created by the week-end guest who lunches every day at his club and has that highly developed passion for puddings peculiar to his class.

While the true Coarse Cook is contemptuous of those cooks whose skill and imagination is restricted to opening tins and boiling up frozen vegetables, he is aware that 'cookery' also includes the preparation and presentation of food that needs no further cooking. Consequently, the store-cupboard is packed stiff with tins balanced on top of each other, which fall over, land on your feet and roll across the kitchen floor whenever you try to get one of them out.

But how else can you stack tins and jars of baked beans, tunny, crab, lobster, consommé, corned beef, artichoke hearts, asparagus tips, sweet corn, shrimps, prawns, salmon, sardines, anchovies, caviar (or lump fish roe if you prefer slumming), button mushrooms, celery, tomatoes, tomato purée, good Bolognese sauce, pimentos, *petits pois*, French beans from Belgium, baby carrots, gherkins, olives, dill cucumber, capers, tomato juice, ham, tongue, devilled ham, liver pâtés, one-kilo jars of Dijon mustard brought back from a French super-market—how else can you stack them, except on top of one another?

And then, no less difficult to balance because they are packed in rectangular boxes of different sizes or small odd-shaped bottles or jars, there are all the condiments, spices and dried herbs which you have collected like a magpie and are sure you will be able to use one day. In desperation after years of failing to find dishes that need the more exotic of them, you have to throw a good pinch of everything into a stew. 'Everything' includes sea salt, celery salt, peppercorns, cloves, cummin seed, coriander seed, powdered cardamom, turmeric, fennel seed, savoury, carraway, mustard seed, pine kernels, dill seed, hot paprika, mild paprika, dried shredded horse-radish, cinnamon, mace, nutmeg, saffron, marjoram, basil, bay leaves, sage, thyme. Thus at one stroke you justify your belief that they would come in useful some-time.

The contents of the store-cupboard listed so far shows very clearly that, unlike the first five ages, the sixth age of Coarse Cooking Man and Woman is one of close and, on the whole, happy collaboration in the kitchen. The man in particular is conscious that he must contribute

more to the partnership than compliments and encouraging
words on his wife's cooking, so he stocks up the store-
cupboard.

This he does by dropping into any promising-looking
delicatessen he sees, and coming out with not just one
tin of poppadums, one packet of fish soup which is mostly
vermicelli, one tin of ladies' fingers, but six of one and
half a dozen of the others. One doesn't want to let the
store-cupboard get too low.

The fact that neither he nor his wife is particularly
fond of the Indian food that would demand poppadums,
or shares the Greeks' delight in ladies' fingers, and that
they long ago swore never to buy that make of starch-
reinforced fish soup again, is irrelevant. You never know
when you might need them.

The husband justifies his tendency to over-stock by
pointing out that nobody ever runs out of things at lunch-
time, when the shops are open, but always in the evening
when they aren't. Therefore it is better to have six of
everything.

Perhaps it is something to do with an inbred feeling of
insecurity, but it is noticeable that when men go shopping
for food they always shop for the future as well as for the
present, as though they wouldn't know where their next
couple of jars of turtle soup were coming from unless
they had a reserve stock of at least another three or four.

This kind of husbandry is easy to mock at, of course (I
knew a man who always kept a gross of scallops in the
fridge in case anybody came to dinner unexpectedly),
but it is nevertheless essential in Coarse Cookery. Then it
has nothing to do with insecurity, only with ensuring
that you have enough of what you want when you want
it. And this is not so easy as you might think.

There is no place in the Organisation of Coarse Cookery
for absent-mindedness or even for simple forgetfulness.
True, these failings are a challenge to the patient's
ingenuity and gift for improvisation, but there is no need
for the Coarse Cook to be faced with situations and
problems which could have been avoided by simple

organisation, one of the most important elements of which is intelligent anticipation.

To illustrate this there is a cautionary tale to be told of a friend of ours, cooking for the first dinner party of her married life. For a first course, she decided to make *œufs en gelée à l'estragon*—eggs in aspic served in ramekin dishes. But when she came to look she had no ramekin dishes, and had never had any. She had visualised for weeks what her first course was going to look like but had neglected to check the dream with the reality. Put out, but not defeated, she resorted to improvisation; she used small soup bowls instead. Unfortunately, when it came to getting the aspic to set, the bowls were too big to go into the fridge, so they were put out on to the window-ledge to cool.

This might have been a satisfactory solution if the window ledge hadn't been in a busy part of central London. By the time the eggs and their aspic were ready to eat they were covered in rich London grime. As it was impossible to remove the black particles from the food, there was nothing for it but to add a lot more black particles, by grinding a generous amount of black pepper over the lot.

Absent-mindedness, or complete failure to organise at all, is paradoxically less catastrophic in its effect than mere imperfect organisation. It causes delay or embarrassment, but not total destruction; it is more often than not the result of what might be called non-cookery.

The worst that can happen is for the cook to have to start doing what she ought to have done an hour before. This happened once with the mother of a friend of ours who, after one glass of Cinzano, went into the kitchen to baste a small turkey she was roasting. After a second (very small) glass of Cinzano she returned to the kitchen to administer another regulation basting. But when she got there the oven was bare. The poor family didn't actually get none—but they had to wait until the cook had removed the turkey from the washing-up machine and put it back in the stove which stood next to it.

The seventh age of Shakespeare's man is matched in the life of Coarse Cooking Man, but thanks to the developments of medicine and dentistry he does not play his last scene of all entirely sans everything, certainly not sans teeth or sans taste. And second childishness? As I have not yet reached this seventh age myself I do not know for sure.

But there is certainly no second childishness about Mr William Ridley, who lives a few miles from us and celebrated his seventieth wedding anniversary only a couple of weeks ago.

'Changes take place all the time,' Mr Ridley told a local reporter, 'but you never stop learning. It wasn't until my ninety-fourth birthday a month ago that I cooked a batch of buns.'

There, I thought, speaks the true Coarse Cook—always trying something for the first time.

Mr Ridley, enjoying his seventh age of cookery, is a noble and encouraging example to us all.

3

Technique

. . . Toil and Trouble
Fire burn and cauldron bubble
SHAKESPEARE

'Six Methods of Cookery are commonly spoken of, viz.,'
said Mrs Beeton, helping her husband to another plateful
of Treacle Pudding (1 lb flour, 8 oz suet, 2 oz breadcrumbs, treacle, grated rind of 1 lemon, 1 tablespoonful
baking powder, salt), '1. Broiling; 2. Roasting; 3. Baking;
4. Boiling; 5. Stewing; 6. Frying.' Other authorities
include also poaching, braising and steaming.

The student of Coarse Cookery needs no reminding that
there are quite a few more methods than the nine listed
above. There is King Alfred the Great's method, for
instance. The most famous Coarse Cook in English
history, apart from Mary Tudor, used to burn cakes
instead of baking them, and we may deduce that they
were not at all bad, either, from the lack of any evidence
to suggest that the cakes were not eaten.

King Alfred's technique will be recognised at once by
his successors in the kitchen as closely related to the process
in Coarse Cookery known as *charbonné*'ing. This, like the
word sauté, comes from the French and means, as a verb,
to char or carbonise.

'*Pommes charbonnées*', for example, are potatoes cooked
to the texture and colour of charcoal. They may be cooked
either in a saucepan, or in a shallow frying pan. If a

'King Alfred's technique will be recognised at once . . .'

saucepan is used, boil the potatoes until all the water has
evaporated and then leave over a full heat until they are a
rich black in colour. Add salt.

When potatoes are *charbonnées* in a frying pan, very
thinly sliced potatoes are fried until the fat is *fumé*, or
heated to give off a black smoke. Continue to fry over
maximum heat. When the potatoes are ready they will
look like slices of black pudding, only darker. Add salt.

One of the greatest advantages of *charbonné*'ing over
other methods of cookery is that what you eat is absolutely
pure and free from any trace of chemical fertilisers and
pesticides. It contains no protein, fat or carbohydrate
of any kind (these are removed by the great heat of the
process), and so is an ideal way of serving up food for
those who have to watch their weight or—particularly—
their digestion. A well *charbonné*'d chop with *charbonnés*

onions, garlic and tomatoes contains nothing to upset the digestion. There is nothing to digest.

But before going into the sophisticated methods of Coarse Cookery, let us look first at the more elementary processes listed by Mrs Beeton and other demagogues.

To begin with let us avoid altogether the use of the term 'broiling'. Apart from anything else, it is extremely difficult for the ever-growing number of English who have as much trouble over the letter 'R' as the Chinese, to make certain that their pronunciation of the word is not mistaken, on account of the similarity of the vowels, for 'boiling'. A confusion of this kind could lead to some unfortunate cookery.

It must be 'grilling', of course. Besides, whoever heard of lunching at the Savoy Broil, or the Broyal Room at the Café Roil? Furthermore, the instrument used in broiling is not a broil, as it is a grill in grilling. It is a gridiron, so if you talked about a Gridiron Room people would think it was a torture chamber at the Tower of London, or American indoor football.

Grilling

Grilling is probably the most popular method among all who practise Coarse Cookery. It is simple, direct, and the smell is nature's greatest aperitif. It needs no skill, only a sense of timing which is quickly acquired with practice, and even more quickly if you don't keep having to cook for people who each want their grills to be done to a different turn.

The most popular guests are those who like their steaks the way you like your own—medium or underdone, perhaps, but never, so long as we cook in English kitchens, 'rare'. Like other Americanisms, 'rare' is used most often by those English who have never been to the States in their lives, but think you will believe they have if they use American terms.

It is a well-known paradox that no Englishman ever went to the United States but that he came back talking and writing better English than before he went. Fleet

Street used to be full of film columnists who wrote as though they had been weaned on *Variety*. When at last they actually went to America they came back and wrote like they was—er, as though they were on *The Times*.

Most people find that a fork is all that's needed to manipulate meat on a grill, provided there is fat to stick the prongs into; otherwise a palette knife is recommended. Some authorities advise using tongs, but their success depends very much on having the right sort of tongs. We had some wooden ones which opened instead of closing when you pressed the handles together. They were one of those fool presents you get at Christmas and we never discovered what they were meant for. Perhaps to pick up dainty cocktail sausages in some dainty finger-crooked way?

Turning the meat on the grill is one of the least of the problems that can face the Coarse Cook nowadays, however. What is far more difficult is to find a modern gas cooker with a grill that is any use at all.

Not so very long ago we foolishly gave up our old cooker and bought what we were assured was the latest technological high-speed marvel. Two or three days after the cooker had been delivered the people who sold it to us telephoned to say that we would be visited by their Domestic Appliances Expert and Cookery Consultant.

We said we were afraid there was nothing she could do; but send her along—if she didn't mind what we said to her.

In due course the young lady arrived.

She said she saw we had a New and Improved De Luxe Model.

Well, we said, it was new. But what was so improved about it?

It had an eye-level grill, she said.

We noticed that, we replied. The eye-level height was 4 ft 2 in., which suggested that it had been designed by a dwarf about 4 ft 7 in. tall, for other dwarfs of the same

B

height. Non-dwarfs, like us, had to bend down to see what the grill was doing.

Furthermore, we continued, what was the use of a grill you couldn't cook a good-sized chop under, unless you first crushed the bones flat so that it didn't catch on fire?

And another point: how was one expected to simmer anything on a stove which went out when you turned the flame down low? With any other stove you could use an asbestos mat, but the instruction book particularly said you mustn't do this. Why?

Our visitor looked embarrassed. 'Well,' she said, 'it's because the heat reflected from the mat isn't good for the enamel round the burners.'

But why not? With the old cooker we'd just got rid of, asbestos mats had been used for years, and nothing had happened to the enamel on *that*.

'No,' said the young lady, 'but I'm afraid the enamel on this cooker isn't quite so good—I mean, so thickly applied, as it was on your old cooker, and it would crack with the terrific New and Improved heat. It's to keep costs down, you know,' she added proudly.

Ignoring her belief that this explained and justified everything, we went on to the next question.

How was one expected to warm plates on the rack over the stove? The famous dwarf's-eye-level grill took up so much room that there was only space for four plates altogether—two soup plates and two meat plates. Obviously the cooker model was designed for romantic tête-à-tête occasions only.

'Oh, but this is where the plates are heated,' said Miss Domestic Appliances Expert and Cookery Consultant of the Year, kneeling on the kitchen floor and opening a cupboard at the bottom of the cooker, under the oven.

We were to turn the oven on and that would warm the plates. It was quite simple, for apparently hot air always went downwards, not upwards, with high-speed gas.

But what if we didn't happen to be using the oven?

Our Cookery Consultant was silent.

'Of course,' she said, brightening, 'you should have

bought the more expensive stove—the New and Improved
Super De Luxe model.'

Did she mean that with the New and Improved *Super*
De Luxe we'd have been able to grill a chop, warm a
dozen plates on the rack and simmer a stew without the
burner going out?

'Oh, no,' she replied. 'All that is the same as this one.
But with the *Super* De Luxe the grill and the oven are
self-igniting too.'

The Domestic Appliance Expert and Cookery Consultant left, sad and puzzled; nobody had ever complained
before. And after all, the firm sold a lot of them.

Which proves only that either people don't mind
inefficient cookers, or feel it is un-English and unsporting
to complain.

'We sell a lot of them.' They'll really have to think up a
new all-purpose bromide soon; even the British public is
beginning to get suspicious.

As a consequence of this ill-designed cooker and its ill-
designed grill we have to use a griddle, corrugated on
one side, flat on the other. It is just as simple to use and
makes just as appetising a smell as a conventional non-
eye-level grill, and is much quieter as it doesn't spit at
everybody.

Roasting

Though we are often assured that roasting is the favourite
national method of cooking it is certainly not the easiest.
Indeed, for the Coarse Cook whose merest entry into a
kitchen is a challenging voyage into the unknown,
roasting is probably the most difficult way of staving off
starvation there is.

In more primitive times, of course, roasting a joint was
simplicity itself: you just fixed it to a spit or a hook over
an open fire and basted it from time to time with the fat
that dripped off into a bowl placed below it. And when it
was done you could see it for yourself, and settle down to
enjoy it forthwith.

But today, with civilisation irrevocably in its stride,

roasting is much more difficult, especially for the Coarse Cook who eschews—i.e. hasn't enough money for—infra-red electronic spits. For us, roasting begins with weighing the meat, then working out how many minutes to the pound it will need before it is done. The oven has to be turned on to the correct temperature.

The meat is put in and the temperature reduced after a given time. Thereafter it is a matter of basting every quarter of an hour and looking at the clock every five seconds or so until the calculated time based on weight × minutes has been reached.

You then take the joint out of the oven, have a messy time trying to pour off the fat to leave some juice behind to make gravy with, and discover when the first slice is cut that the inside of the meat is quite blue. You reckon this must be due to faulty arithmetic and put the joint back in the oven.

As the oven has been turned off for some time you start it up again at its hottest, then put the joint back into it at once for ten minutes. It comes out a dark leathery brown, and you realise that you should have basted it. But basting, you have been told, is necessary only every fifteen minutes and it was back in the oven for only ten. You can't win, can you?

The only thing to do now is to consult the list of Excuses and Explanations included later in this manual and thank heaven that at least you'd picked on a good bottle of wine to have with the roast, reflecting at the same time that your great-grandfather could have done the meat to a turn without once looking at the clock, or thinking of temperatures.

But then, what *he* was doing was roasting. What you've been doing all this time is in fact baking, and you just happen to be lucky that all the engineering and manipulation and calculations required to bake a joint result in something that looks *faintly* like what our ancestors called a roast.

Baking

Considering that when you thought you were roasting you were technically baking all the time, the straight-forward process of baking, and knowing you are baking with the intention of baking, ought to be child's play when you come to it. It probably *is* child's play, but knowing the complicated things children play with nowadays that's not going to be much comfort to the likes of you and me.

Certainly, baking to bake is a more relaxed method of cookery than baking to roast. There isn't all that clock-watching and basting and pouring off of fat without burning yourself, for a start. The only real trouble is to decide what you want to bake and, having decided, to muster enough skill and self-confidence to be able to prepare it. And—most important—if you decide against baking at the last moment, whether there is any other reasonably easy way of serving it up.

Baking can be an ambiguous aid to cookery. At one end of the scale it can produce the most perfect, trouble-free product of the oven—the potato baked in its jacket. At the other end it raises serious doubts about Mrs Beeton's claim that while cookery can render the potato harmless and fit for human consumption it can also do the same for the manioc, which is 'poisonous when gathered'.

The manioc, or cassava, is a plant grown in the West Indies and South America, and for all that Mrs Beeton brackets it with the potato, it is hardly likely that she served it up as a vegetable at her dining table. All it does for a living is provide starch from its roots for making cassava bread, and tapioca. Whether or not Mrs Beeton's cooking of tapioca actually rendered it harmless to pets and children, I do not know, but it certainly could not have made it fit for normal human consumption.

Within reason baking is a method that does not make too great a demand on the attention once the process of cooking has begun, but the preparation of food for baking often needs an unexpected amount of care.

You would hardly think you could go far wrong with an

elementary item like jacket potatoes, for instance, but you can. Until I learnt to pierce the skins all over with a fork before putting them in the oven, there were regularly noisy explosions as the potatoes burst open and more or less disintegrated at precisely the moment one wanted to serve them. I can't imagine how I hadn't heard about this sooner; it would have saved a lot of scraping off of potato fragments from the sides and floor of the oven if I had.

One thing is definite about baking: it is a process which will make an awful mess of the oven, if it possibly can, making no allowances for the human failing of the cook. That same friend of ours whose mother, you will remember, put the turkey in the washing-up machine, also had an aunt who left her mark on the annals of Coarse Cookery.

When she was first married she set out to make a rice pudding. She had never seen a recipe for it, but it was so obviously simple that she followed her instinct. Rice puddings had always tasted to her like rice and milk, so she put a pound of rice in the dish, added a pint of milk to it, and put in the oven. An hour later she came back into the kitchen, opened the oven door, and was surprised to find it filled with a slow-moving mass of white lava.

Baking is unrivalled, however, as a means of refurbishing all the damp peanuts, potato crisps, *canapé* biscuits, cheese straws, and those other stale morsels which get brought out and dusted off for occasional Sunday morning visitors to munch with their drinks. What is left over on these occasions is put back into the cupboard to recover its dampness and to continue ageing in peace for another time, when they are put into the oven once again for an overhaul.

Boiling

According to Mrs Beeton, 'Boiling is generally thought to be the easiest method of cooking,' and she goes on to tell us—I suspect because she secretly fancied herself as a scientist—that water boils at above 100°C or 212°F if

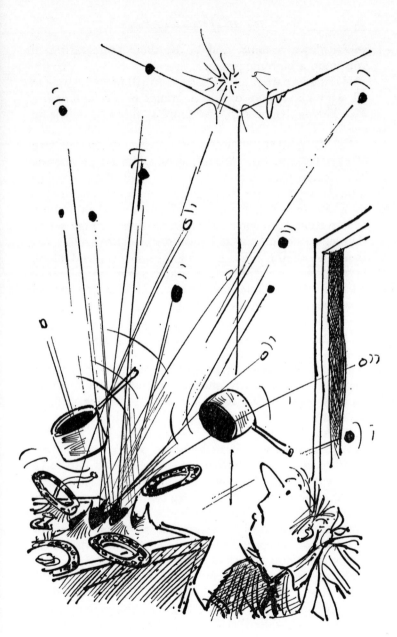

'You would hardly think you could go far wrong with
jacket potatoes . . .'

you're down a mine, and below those temperatures if you're up a high mountain.

Having imparted information that will be invaluable to all who make pots of tea in mines or on mountains, Mrs Beeton assures us: 'The simplest thing to boil is an egg.'

I shall be dealing more particularly with the cooking of eggs later in this chapter; meanwhile let us just ask Mrs Beeton where on earth she got hold of an idea like that. To say that 'the simplest thing' to boil is an egg is to show an appalling ignorance of eggs and their nature.

For some who have led sheltered lives it may sound simple, but for others (as I related earlier) to boil an egg is not at all the simplest thing. Among the rest of us, indeed, the successful boiling of an egg can sometimes be an almost impossible achievement. That is because we have to reckon with the character of the chicken that laid the egg.

Our weekly supply of really good, fat, new-laid eggs comes from the butcher, who sells eggs from a real free-range chicken farm. There is only one thing wrong with them: the shells nearly always crack when I boil them. As they regularly did this when put into boiling water, I tried putting them into cold water and bringing it to the boil. At the moment the water boiled the eggs still exploded, and, as before, the white poured out of them into the saucepan, where it was poached and had to be skimmed off before it boiled over and put the gas out.

I still think that boiling an egg from cold is a less risky process in the end, but it is obvious that nothing can be done to guard against the organic shortcomings of the chickens whose constant laying of eggs with brittle shells is obviously due to lack of important items in their diet, such as hop manure, wine vinegar and kaolin. Odd, nevertheless, that the eggs my wife boils never explode.

There are, in fact, very much simpler things to boil than an egg—vegetables that don't have to be lowered gently into the saucepan in case they crack, which don't explode and put out the gas flame. But even so, boiling is far from being the foolproof method of cooking that we are expected to believe. Too soon one learns that though water boils at 212°F it is expected to do so in vessels of many different shapes and sizes, and at varying speeds of ebullition—fast, furious, slow, medium and simmering. The last speed is the most difficult of all, because it either boils too hard or goes off the boil altogether and so becomes almost as much of a bore to supervise as roasting.

The shape of vessels for boiling in may seem irrelevant, but where an oven is an oven, and a grill (except on the New and Improved) is a grill, saucepans and pots have to be found which will hold anything from a globe artichoke or a cauliflower, to a pound of spinach or a pound of unbroken spaghetti.

Some pots are so shaped that they will hold what you want to boil, but not enough water to do it with; others will hold the water but are the wrong shape for what you want to boil with it.

Then there is the question of the right lids for the saucepans, and, if you haven't got lids that will fit, the long-term question of the condensation on your kitchen walls which follows as a result.

I daresay Mrs Beeton might claim that the second easiest thing to boil is potatoes. Here again she would be lucky, for only the very privileged ever get the potatoes the rest of us feel we deserve—potatoes that cook in the time they ought to and don't keep everybody waiting for dinner. Instead, we get potatoes that suddenly collapse in a mush when three minutes earlier the centres were as hard as raw swedes.

I daresay a lot of this has to do with the variety of potato you pick on, but of all the everyday processes of Coarse Cookery the boiling of potatoes is the most unpredictable. The chanciness of the whole affair, indeed, probably explains why, as Boy Scouts, we were not given potato-boiling as part of our cooking test. The psychological effect of failure at that early age could have been wholesale defection from the Movement (though where I was at school conscientious objection to joining the

Scouts was not recognised), and the Chief Scout in his wisdom realised that whatever a small boy did to a couple of sausages in a billy-can, nothing would deter him from eating and enjoying them in the end. You couldn't count on that with potatoes.

However much boiling may be 'generally thought to be the easiest method of cookery', to a great many of us it is a process whose equivocal nature is perfectly reflected in the familiar saying, 'A watched pot never boils.' It depends on whether you want the pot to boil or not to boil. Taken one way it has all the characteristic jokiness of the nursery proverb. A saucepan of milk never boils until you turn your back on it, then it boils over. But taken another way it is perfectly true. This is when you are engaged in the rather deceptive business of simmering.

With this method the ingredients are put into cold water, which is gently brought to the boil, but never allowed to exceed boiling point. In fact, the experts even go so far as to tell you that simmering temperature is from 180° to 210°F; and a nice tricky performance this can be, too—gauging the exact moment when the liquid reaches 211° and the temperature must be reduced. To ensure that in these circumstances a pot never boils, it has to be watched with obsessive care.

A very two-faced kind of cliché, that one about watched pots.

Stewing

If boiling is not necessarily the easiest method of cookery, it is certainly easier than stewing. Food boiled by even the most abject beginner is occasionally edible, if often rather dull. Food stewed by the complete culinary ignoramus is nearly always revolting and often downright dangerous. It is only when he has graduated in his craft the hard way, after long clinical experience, that the Coarse Cook learns that there is more to the process of stewing than ends up on a plate.

And yet, on first thoughts, there could surely be nothing simpler than cutting up bits of meat and vegetables and throwing them all into a pot and simmering them until they are done. This is the view almost universally held by the lowest grade of beginners in the kitchen.

Most beginners develop into Coarse Cooks or High Cooks; in either case they soon change their original views on stewing. There are some, however, who remain beginners all their long lives. My mother is one of those.

When one talks of 'memorable' meals it is usually of rare dishes and unforgettable wines. But memories can be of both good and evil and no meal has ever been more disastrously memorable to me than one that included a lamb stew cooked by my mother.

I was a small boy and on the point of catching a late train back to boarding school on the last day of the holidays. For an early supper a plate of breast of lamb stew was put in front of me, and without thinking I ate a spoonful. It was the last mouthful I ate that night. What felt like boiling oil burned my tongue so violently that I carried the searing wounds for weeks and the unfading memory of them to this day. My mother has always considered that to skim off the fat would in some way deprive the stew of all its nutritional value.

The experience, to say the least in the most fashionable way, was traumatic. Thereafter I avoided the only dish in my mother's repertoire by demanding an egg, or bread and jam. I excused myself by muttering that I was observing the meatless day demanded by the rigorous course of training demanded by the forthcoming cricket/ rugby/athletics term at school. The only saving grace of being at an English boarding school was the freedom from my mother's cooking which it offered for about 255 days of the year. School cooking was nauseating, it is true; but it didn't cause actual bodily harm like Mum's home cooking in my family.

The Coarse Cook, then, skims all the fat from the stew. This is in accordance with his centuries-old principles that he cooks to be able to eat and enjoy what he cooks, and is what distinguishes him from the eternal beginner.

Some forms of stewing, indeed, take the Coarse Cook

into the realms of *haute cuisine* itself—as, for instance, when meat is browned by quick frying to seal the juices before putting it into the stew pot with the vegetables. The process is necessary with Oxtail Stew, but not—and I am supported by the highest authorities in this—with Irish Stew.

This makes life much easier.

Frying

We are concerned here with frying as a process in its own right and not, as when meat is browned for stewing, as a stage in another process.

There is no doubt that frying is a very popular method of cooking, and largely, I believe, because it gets quick results before your very eyes. It involves no clock-watching, you don't have to keep opening an oven or lifting a lid to see how it's getting on. You just keep your eye firmly fixed on what's in the frying pan and prod it from time to time if you must—though not if it's an egg.

Frying is a pleasantly busy way of cooking. It bubbles busily, it makes a busy noise. It is not only busy in itself, but the cause of busyness in others. It is the inspiration of the one proverb that is at all true to commonplace every-day life in the kitchen. Half one's frying life is spent trying to avoid the accident of letting food slip out of the frying pan into the fire.

While it confirms one proverb, frying also contradicts another. Frying not only permits, but demands, the creation of smoke without fire. Indeed, as with the American Indians, smoke is a signal to begin operations: blue smoke for get ready, grey smoke for get set, and black smoke for go.

The traditionalist who has a cooker and doesn't like nature being mucked about with, can prove that there is no smoke without fire easily enough. He turns up the heat until the fat in the frying pan is really hot, then he takes a handful of sliced potatoes which have been in water and throws them into the pan. The result is a remarkable display of apparently spontaneous combustion

'The result is a remarkable display. . . .'

with flames two feet high, and clouds of smoke billowing all over the kitchen. There is little danger attached to this process, as long as you are suitably dressed; quick removal of the pan from the stove will prevent the flames spreading and the smoke rendering visibility altogether nil.

If there are some who regard the demonstration of the theory of No Smoke Without Fire as a trivial, childish exhibition, let me please remind them that the result of the traditionalist's experiment is a legitimate and indeed classic method of cookery. It is the method that produces dishes known as *flambés*. True, our traditionalist's potatoes are not likely to be edible, but the principle of setting ingredients on fire is no less valid for that.

While food that is *flambé* is not always the product of the frying pan, it was food that was being *sauté* that first jumped from the frying pan into the fire. The lack of an equivalent English word for *sauté* leads to some appalling attempts to make an English verb out of a French adjective—'after sautéing', 'when it is sauté'd', 'first sauté the potatoes'. This literally translated would lead to phrases like 'after jumpeding', 'when it is jumpeded', 'first jumped the potatoes'. The term 'sautéing' (what else *can* one say?) is a little misleading if one exaggerates its connection with jumping.

The most frequent one-way traffic between frying pan and fire in the end comes, of course, from tossing—a method of frying recommended only to those with the eye and dexterity of a juggler who are devoted to pancakes.

For the less agile, sautéing is the most painless way. Not too much smoke, an occasional shake of the hand, and it will cook almost anything you can think of.

For many bachelor years I had a deep-frying pan with a basket, not for chips, but in the hope that one day I would succeed in producing those delicious tiny fried whole potatoes about the size of a ping-pong ball which you get in restaurants in Italy. I never did succeed; the potatoes always came out looking a treat, but bone hard underneath the appetising brown exterior.

There remains one further process of cooking which

might count as frying. This is known as sweating. However, I am not altogether sure that the method of sweating vegetables—cooking them very slowly in butter in a pan with the lid on until they are soft—is not a little on the grand (or *haute*) side for the average Coarse Cook. At any rate, it needs considerable care and skill in adjusting the heat to ensure that the vegetables do not cook too fast and so end up as a burnt and unpalatable mess which even the English, who are expert in ruining vegetables, find inedible.

Steaming and Poaching

These are extremely 'sophisticated' methods of cooking—that is 'worldly-wise', if we are to believe the dictionary, or just 'advanced', which is what scientists mean when they meddle with the English vocabulary.

An interruption. Did I never tell you of that notorious Marlborough Street court case, in the early 1940s? Let me quote from the *News of the World*:

> Asked by the magistrate if she knew the meaning of the word 'unsophisticated', Miss Dawn replied: 'I don't know. Someone who is not a prostitute, I suppose.'

I hoped at the time that this had finally put the term in its place, but it hadn't.

The process of steaming, of course, is not so much 'sophisticated' as used in the cooking of rather 'sophisticated' food. Things, I mean, like sauces. Equally, it is used for the cooking of food which has nothing but the lowest plebeian and nursery associations—like suet puddings and custard, and tasteless, health-giving fish.

Steaming will certainly produce lovely scrambled eggs, but so will an ordinary saucepan. It's a matter of choice. Both ways mean messy washing-up.

Poaching is another method with 'sophisticated' overtones. What We consider poaching and what They consider poaching are two very different things. To us only one thing is ever poached and that is an egg. There are two ways of doing this, both rather tricky.

The classic way of poaching an egg is to stir up a whirl-pool in a saucepan of boiling water and drop the egg into it. In order to prevent the white of the egg disintegrating into ribbons with the centrifugal force, it is customary to add a tablespoonful of vinegar, or a teaspoonful of lemon juice, to a pint of water. Whatever the exact chemical processes may be, I do not know, but the acid keeps the white in order.

Like too many classic methods of doing anything nowadays, whirlpool-poaching is growing rarer. The last time I encountered it in public I could have done without it. British Railways served up some poached eggs in which one tablespoonful of water had apparently been added to a pint of vinegar.

Why the restaurant car didn't use one of those patent contraptions like a mould for scones, which the rest of us poach eggs in, was obvious. Being unlike the rest of us, British Railways knew that in order to get a poached egg out of these moulds you have to butter them first, and they were being mean with the butter.

They were, in fact, showing quite a degree of 'sophistication'. The Coarse Cook never remembers about buttering the mould until the egg is cooked. Then it is as solid as a bun and he tries to dig it out and finds it is stuck fast.

The poached egg is poaching in its most elementary form, and about as high as any average Coarse Cook should aim. Once you start poaching poultry and fish you have one foot on the bottom rung of the wrong ladder. Furthermore, you'll never again really want to eat either of these things done in any other way, and it can involve a lot of sauce-making as well.

Pot Roasting

Finally, there is this rather satisfactory method which combines a bit of frying, a bit of sweating, a bit of stewing, and a bit of roasting in one more or less fool-proof process. The frying is to brown the meat, the sweating is to soften the bed of vegetables you lay the meat on, the stewing of everything in its own juice is what goes on once you put the lid on the casserole, and the roasting cooks it.

Like the sweating of vegetables, however, pot roasting is only for those Coarse Cooks who have a well-developed gift of patience in the kitchen. I know that patience and the Art of Coarse Cookery sound like a serious contradiction in terms, but both are recognised virtues, and the possession of two virtues is not altogether unheard of. Even Members of Parliament have been known (1) to hold their tongues, and (2) to retire.

Any attempt to speed up the process of pot roasting by raising the heat above the gentle minimum it requires can be a disaster. That is, unless you like the rich toffee which is all that's left at the bottom of the casserole as a result of your impatience.

Personally I do, so I am content whichever way the pot roast turns out.

HORS-D'ŒUVRE AND FIRST COURSES

If, for some reason, the Coarse Cook should ever lose his enthusiasm for his Art and everything to do with it, there would be no need for him either to starve or to spend a fortune eating out. He could quite easily live off hors-d'œuvre for the rest of his life, and enjoy every mouthful of it.

The nutritional value of hors-d'œuvre is something the impecunious young have always recognised. In our own earlier days Soho restaurants were patronised and recommended entirely according to the generosity of the helpings and the variety of choice of the hors-d'œuvre. With a plate of spaghetti after it and half a carafe of rough red you could eat yourself to a standstill very cheaply indeed—by the standards of the time, that is, not just in comparison with the prices of today's inflation.

A spread of hors-d'œuvre in the home, of course, need

involve little preparation and none of the cookery that a restaurant has to put into its confection. So the disillusioned, disgruntled, incapacitated, or just downright idle Coarse Cook can survive quite happily, as long as he knows of a good delicatessen and buys his tins wisely.

It must be admitted, however, that the English tend to be a little greedy about their hors-d'œuvre; perhaps it is the result of their impecunious youth. The Coarse Cook will, I hope, suppress this national enthusiasm for hors-d'œuvre and limit the number of items beginning a meal to three or four at the most.

Nevertheless, if an hors-d'œuvre is to have any charm, as much of it as possible ought to be prepared by the Coarse Cook himself, and in one branch of his Art he can, and must, set the rest of the country an example in gracious eating. That is in the preparation and presentation of tomatoes, cucumbers and beetroot.

Tomatoes

The English catering industry (which, of course, is little concerned with cooking, still less with eating) considers it has done all that anybody can ask for, if raw tomatoes are served cut in quarters with the tough skin on. In provincial hotels, pubs, boarding houses, tea shoppes, caffs and kayffs, and restaurants boasting 'continental cuisine' (which continent?) all over the British Isles, these unappealing wedges of tomato are included in the salad you have particularly asked should be green. They are also used to garnish plates of cold meat, fish, or eggs with bottled mayonnaise. Their main purpose, one can only suppose, must be decorative; they are rarely worth eating.

The Coarse Cook prepares and cooks food to eat, not to stare at. So no tomato ever appears at his table which has not been properly skinned, sliced and dressed.

The process is simple. Put the tomatoes in a bowl, nick the skins with a sharp knife, and pour boiling water over them. If the tomatoes are ripe the skins will pull off after about fifteen seconds (or almost as long as it takes to

sing the first sixteen bars of 'Land of Hope and Glory').
If they are underripe they will take longer (add the
chorus of 'Rule, Britannia' to 'Land of Hope and Glory').

Cut the tomatoes into thin slices, put them in a dish,
add olive oil, season (as they say) to taste, and serve. If
you can lay hands on any basil, chop some and sprinkle
it over the tomatoes; failing basil, chopped chives. Or a
few rings of raw shallot with chopped parsley to protect
you from the dyspeptic effect of the shallot. The result
looks like, tastes like, and is, a proper tomato salad.

Cucumbers

The English have two unshakable beliefs about cucumber:
(1) that if you leave the skin on you will not get indigestion, and (2) that if you take the skin off you will not
get indigestion.

The first belief is held by half the country's public and
home caterers who, in order to ensure that plenty of peel
is included in each mouthful, cut cucumber in slices as
thick as fifty-penny pieces. The cucumber is then eaten
with bottled 'salad cream', or soaked in malt vinegar,
when it is known as cucumber salad.

The second belief is held by the other half of the
country's public and home caterers who, in order to ensure
that the peel is seen clearly to have been removed, cut
cucumber in slices as thick as two fifty-penny pieces. It is
then eaten with bottled 'salad cream', or soaked in malt
vinegar, when it is known as cucumber salad.

In their anxiety to attribute eupeptic or dyspeptic
properties to the skin of the cucumber, neither group of English cucumber-eaters gives much thought to the cucumber
itself. It does not occur to them, as it does to any Coarse
Cook, that by peeling the cucumber, slicing it as thinly
as possible, leaving it well salted for an hour to draw out
the water, draining it, and dressing it with olive oil, the
cucumber should be rendered completely digestible.

If by some awful chance you still cannot subdue the
cucumber, eat half a dozen radishes *and their leaves*. The
leaves have a remarkable effect, suppressing not only all

repetition of the radishes, but of anything else you may eat at the same meal. Including cucumber.

Well, it works for me, anyway.

Beetroot

It would be interesting to know how the English became so passionately fond of vinegar with everything that they can only just be restrained from pouring it into their tea. And malt vinegar at that. Admittedly, the making of native wine vinegar has been a bit difficult in a country without native vineyards for so long, but why on earth has it taken so long for the rediscovery of cider vinegar? After all, it isn't as though apples didn't grow on trees.

Beetroot, even more than fish and chips, suffers in England from malt vinegar. It also suffers from being obstinately difficult to buy uncooked. For some reason the average greengrocer's customers are unable to boil beetroot for themselves, so it is sold ready cooked. (Why only beetroot? They don't sell ready-cooked anything else.)

As an inevitable development of this helplessness, supermarkets and others sell beetroot already peeled and wrapped in cellophane, and apparently stewed in malt vinegar.

The answer to a problem like this, if you have a garden, is, of course, to grow your own. You can then cook them when they are the size of new potatoes and eat them either hot with no dressing at all except butter, or diced (*not* sliced, for a change) and served with olive oil and chopped shallots and parsley. Or with finely chopped onion or chives, if you can't get shallots. But always with parsley.

But if you can't get shallots or raw beetroot then a campaign must be launched to get them into the shops.

We managed to get aubergines and courgettes and fennel into the shops after years of constant nagging. We ought to be able to do the same for raw beetroot and shallots. After all, they do grow here; they don't have to be imported.

Apart from boiling the beetroot, you will notice that so far the Coarse Cook has involved himself in no cookery at

'. . . passionately fond of vinegar with everything . . .'

all. Nor has he had to resort to ready-to-serve store-bought fare, and the longer he can resist that temptation the better he and his guests will eat.

Also (and this is a very important aspect of Coarse Cookery), the preparation of good hors-d'œuvre in his own kitchen makes the Coarse Cook look as if he has been cooking with great skill, whereas in fact he has been been doing no cooking at all. This is particularly the case with some of the fish dishes which you will never find in a delicatessen, but which are remarkably easy to prepare, effective to show off and delicious to eat.

The easiest of all is *Haddok anglais fumé au citron,* or (you would be right to assume) smoked haddock with lemon. Recipe: remove the backbone of a large lightly smoked haddock, being careful not to damage the flesh more than you can help. Slice it as you would slice a side of smoked salmon (if you had one), and squeeze plenty of lemon juice over it. Then leave it for an hour or two and serve it up with wedges of lemon, and brown bread and butter.

Even less likely sounding as an appetiser than raw smoked haddock is probably raw kippers marinated in oil. All you want to prepare a dish that can taste almost as good as smoked salmon is a packet of kipper fillets, a finely sliced onion, bay leaves and olive oil.

You skin the fillets and cut them into slices. Lay them in a dish (with high sides to it like a soufflé dish) and between each layer of fish put some finely sliced onion and a small piece of bay leaf. Pour enough olive oil over this to cover it.

Put a lid or a piece of tinfoil over the dish and leave it in a cool place for a day, perhaps two days. When you are ready to eat it, spear the fish with a fork and shake the oil off it before putting it on your plate. Then sprinkle it with black pepper and a good squeeze of lemon.

So long as they are completely covered with oil, kippers done in this way will keep in the fridge for months on end.

Finally—because three virtuoso fish dishes are enough for any Coarse Cook's repertoire—there is the Bismark Herring.

Take the following ingredients:

A very large jar of pickled dill cucumbers
Four cleaned and filleted herrings with the skins left on
One large onion, finely sliced

The first thing to do is to eat all the dill cucumber, but keep the screw-top jar and the liquid that came in it.

Into the jar place a layer of fish (a helpful fishmonger will have done all the cleaning and filleting for you), then a layer of finely sliced onion. Then a layer of fish, then a layer of onion. Keep this up until the jar is full or you've run out of fish, whichever is the sooner. If the liquid needs topping up to cover the fish, pour in enough of a solution of equal parts of wine or cider vinegar and water. If you don't eat them at once, they will keep in the fridge for several days.

On the other hand, if you don't want to buy a large jar of pickled dill cucumbers all that much, then you can make the pickling liquor yourself. But that involves recipe books and things.

Unless you have married a good cook who makes them, the cooking of pâtés is not something one should encourage in the Coarse Kitchen. It is, frankly, a rather difficult and lengthy business, demanding more patience, and even skill, than is usually possessed by the average Coarse Cook.

There are, however, ways of producing pâté without having to open a tin—a regrettable practice, since no matter what the label says, the contents of one cheap tin tastes of exactly the same peppery preservative as the next. (It is really a question of class and quality, of course. Some of the best pâté de foie gras I have ever tasted did in fact come out of a tin imported from Strasbourg. It was authentic enough to have come out of a terrine.)

The easiest home-made pâté I know of is called *Pâté Clarence*. It gets its name from a pub in the Old Brompton Road which was a regular meeting place in South Kensington for musicians, painters, actors, Rugby internationals, Welsh singers, secret service agents, and a number of local well-educated cheque-bouncers.

The basis of this pâté is gorgonzola and it evolved when one of the customers at the Clarence, who wanted a change from the only foreign cheese known to pubs in those days, tried mashing into his gorgonzola a few drops of Worcestershire sauce. Next time he added celery salt and a thimbleful of sherry to the mixture, and in a little while he had half the pub mixing and mashing with tomato ketchup, olive oil, French mustard, pepper, Guinness, H.P. Sauce, pickles and the juice from pickled onions.

The inventor himself limited the flavouring of his cheese

to Worcestershire sauce (occasionally substituted with French mustard) and celery salt; sometimes port, Marsala or Madeira were used instead of the sherry. And it is in this form that the recipe has come down in our family. It makes a good spread—but spread very thinly—to eat on French bread at the beginning of the meal, or on toast as a savoury at the end of it. If the flavour of the gorgonzola is a bit fierce, mix cream cheese with it until it is tamed.

The Clarence, where this pâté came from, I now remember was the source of a minor gastronomic tragedy in my early life. One of the many chauffeurs who came in to play darts in the evenings worked for an enormously rich employer, and after one particularly lavish party had been given a present by the butler of a pound jar of caviar. The chauffeur had taken it home and after one mouthful decided it tasted too strongly of fish for his liking. He brought the jar round to the Clarence and asked me if I'd like it. I said I would, and he gave me the lot. But would I please promise to return the jar. The butler could get 1s 6d back on it. I promised to do this and took the caviar home.

Instead of obeying my instincts and wolfing the whole lot at one sitting, I ate only a little and decided to make the rest last. This frugality might have been all right if I'd had a fridge to keep the jar in, but I hadn't and all but a couple of modest helpings of the caviar went bad.

The butler collected his 1s 6d on the jar, however.

SOUPS

Soup of the evening, beautiful soup!
OLD LEWIS CAROL

Too many cooks, the saying goes, spoil the broth. By which we have always been expected to understand that too many cooks working at the same time on the same broth are likely to spoil it. It might be a more convincing maxim if anybody had ever bothered to define

exactly how many cooks are too many, and what it is they
do to spoil what kind or size of broth. As nobody has ever
done this one can only suppose that what is meant is that
there are too many cooks who spoil broth. This is much
more likely, but there is no reason why the Coarse Cook
should be among them.

In Coarse Cookery there is only one broth, anyway,
and not even an inattentive Boy Scout could do much to
spoil it, short of forgetting to put water in the pot.

'Broth', of course, is really soup. Which makes me
wonder more than ever about too many cooks spoiling it.
At its dictionary-best, broth is water that meat has been
boiled in.

Coarse Soup comes, as they say, in three forms: thick,
when it is *potage*; clear, when it is *consommé*; and *au
naturel*, when you finish up with a plate full of vegetable
and animal matter some of which floats, much of which
doesn't, and most of which is likely to choke you if you
don't watch every mouthful.

This *spécialité* of the *soir* may be made from any two or
all of the following ingredients (strike out what is not
applicable):

Leeks	Bones
Onions	Beetroot
Red, white, green cabbage	Lettuce
Garlic	Peas
Potato	Lentils
Carrots	Broad beans
Turnips	French beans
Courgettes	Dried white Italian beans
Barley	Tomatoes
Celery	Diced bacon
Watercress	Celeriac

A spoonful of Bovril, a small packet of stock cubes,
salt, a spoonful of Marmite, peppercorns, spinach
water, bean water, cabbage water, asparagus water
(in season)

Cut up everything into small pieces and boil very

slowly in a large saucepan with the lid on until it is done.

To end up with a *potage* pass the contents of the sauce-pan through a sieve. If you favour a *consommé* separate the liquid from the vegetables by straining. For straight-forward soup *au naturel* don't do anything at all beyond being careful not to slop everything about when you ladle the soup and vegetables into the consumers' plates.

This basic Coarse Soup is sometimes known as Father's Fancy or Dad's Delight, owing to its popularity among men both sides of the stove, as it were. Easy to cook, easy to eat. That is Coarse Cookery in a theoretical nutshell.

One really ought to be able to do the same sort of thing with fish—filling a pot with the dozens of different fish found around our coasts. The trouble with this is that most of the fish caught in this country seems far too good to make soup of, and if you use only the heads and tails and bones of the fish you normally eat you'd have to get through a terrible lot of fish before you had enough bits to make into soup. We do not all have the reserves of Madame Prunier, unfortunately.

For some reason, the dehydrated soup manufacturers—or rather, the manufacturers of dehydrated soup—have not yet managed to think up a fish soup that isn't stiff with vermicelli or cornflour. No doubt there is some subtle chemical justification for this, but who wants pasta in fish soup? Even in Italy fish soup is free of this irrelevance.

None of this, however, need stop the diligent Coarse Cook making a good home-made Bouillabaisse, using fillets of local fish like coley (formerly rock salmon), cod, plaice, fresh haddock, mackerel, herring or other 'meaty' fish, where the Mediterranean recipe demands special Mediterranean fish with special Mediterranean bones to choke you with.

To save you getting out of your chair and looking for the book I got it out of, the recipe goes like this:

Cut up your English fish into pieces about an inch square. Into a casserole pour about one glass of olive oil,

'. . . can be made from any two, or all of the
following . . .'

and a glass of dry white wine (which is considered a heresy by the experts, but very tasty by the consumer and who's eating this stew anyway?). Heat the oil and wine with chopped onions, garlic, parsley, tomatoes, a bay leaf, fennel, a piece of dry orange peel, black pepper, a good pinch of all-spice and a few coriander seeds.

When this mixture is hot, add the fish, a pinch of salt and a good pinch of saffron. Cover with water and boil until everything is cooked.

Put slices of French bread into the bottom of a soup tureen and pour the bouillabaisse over it.

If you think a filleted bouillabaisse is lacking in the essential hazards of the authentic fish stew, fish bones can be added before serving.

It is not generally known that bouillabaisse was invented by the patron saint of cooks, St Martha, whose feast day is celebrated on July 29 by Coarse Cooks all over the eating world.

One of Martha's exploits was the slaying of a dragon near Marseilles. The Marseillais, being a frugal people, salvaged the corpse of the dragon, boiled it in sea water with saffron and liked it so much that they have been trying to repeat the dish ever since. As dragons have declined in number since those days, however, spiny lobster, sea urchins and other hideous-looking, dragon-like substitutes have had to be used as ingredients instead.

'Bouillabaisse' is believed to be a Provençal corruption of the Italian *boiessa*, meaning the hangman's wife, or *bugliolobasso*, meaning a low-lying earth closet. Few etymologists and no entomologists accept these derivations, however.

The fascination of soup for the Coarse Cook is that it can be made of anything. It can be substantial enough for a main dish, or no more than flavoured water to give you an appetite. It can warm you; it can keep you cool; it can act as food and drink together. Alexandre Dumas has a recipe for a beer soup which contains the following ingredients:

3 quarts of beer	3 oz of sugar
Half a glass of rum	A zest of lemon
Half a glass of hock	5 oz of butter
A piece of preserved ginger	5 oz of flour
A piece of cinnamon	15 raw egg-yolks
Another 7 oz of butter	

Dumas specifies 'light beer, pale or brown' which, since the soup is described as *à la Berlinoise,* means that fizzy beer will do. Whether our present-day fizzy English draught beer will do, I do not know. But ideally, bitter or mild, or in the winter, strong ale, all drawn from the wood, are what should be used.

The process—so Dumas thinks—is simple. Make a light paste of the butter and flour in a pot (in case you don't know it, you are now cooking a *roux*). Stir it and cook it for a few moments. Before it can change colour add the beer and stir till it boils. Put it on one side for twenty-five minutes, then skim it.

Meanwhile, put the rum and the hock, the preserved ginger, cinnamon, sugar and lemon into a small pot. Put a cover on it and keep it warm.

When you've skimmed it, thicken the soup with the egg yolks. Strain it and add the second lot of butter in small pieces, then the strained stew-up of spiced rum-and-wine. Decant the mixture into a tureen and serve with slices of toast.

Though Dumas doesn't say so (any more than he tells us how many people he thinks he's cooking for), this soup is capable of many variations—like using mild-and-bitter, or lager, draught stout or audit ale, more rum or red wine with dark beer, adding cloves, garlic and aromatic peppercorns; and more rum.

Of course, if you can't be bothered with all that paste and egg-yolk thickening, you can leave them out. Serve the soup in glasses and you have, among other things, a perfectly good mulled ale.

Scandinavian cookery includes several alcoholic soups, among them a fish soup with Marsala. The Danes (with

their *Öllebröd*) and the Norwegians (with their *Øllebrod*) have beer soups, but nothing like so interesting as *soupe à la Berlinoise* and so hardly worth the Coarse Cook's while to look into.

On the whole, the few Scandinavians I have known have always had better ways of dealing with alcohol than pouring it into soup. Especially at breakfast.

EGGS

An egg is full of meat
SHAKESPEARE

 As we have already seen, in discussing the basic methods of cookery (pp. 30 et seq.), though boiled eggs may be regarded by some as the easiest things to boil, boiling is far from being the easiest way to cook an egg.

My own experience is that frying an egg is attended by fewer hazards—always allowing that there are at least three first-rate opportunities of ruining the egg in the process: breaking the yolk when you first break the egg into a cup to avoid breaking the egg (and to see it isn't bad, as well); breaking the yolk when you pour the egg out of the cup into the frying pan to avoid breaking the yolk by pouring the egg direct from shell to frying pan; and breaking the yolk when you lift the egg out of the frying pan onto your plate.

I know the only mishap that usually occurs in boiling an egg is that the shell cracks or explodes, but this, I maintain, is something over which nobody has any control. In frying an egg, however, the possible mishaps listed above are entirely the cook's fault. But they can, of course, be avoided with practice and care.

The most difficult trick of all in frying eggs need not concern the Coarse Cook, because he will instinctively not try to perform it. This is the frying of eggs on both sides, called by the Americans 'Over Easy'.

Except as a means of destroying all the appetising appearance and personality of eggs cooked 'Sunny Side Up', by making them look as if they were poached, this method will strike the Coarse Cook as peculiarly pointless, having neither aesthetic attraction nor culinary advantage.

A fried egg is a fried egg, we always say, and it was never intended to hide its beautiful face behind a white veil of bitumen and water.

The aesthetic appeal of a boiled egg is much more a matter of controversial opinion. In this country people pay extra to get brown eggs. In the United States they pay extra not to. Why one Anglo-Saxon's egg should be another Anglo-Saxon's poison has never been explained. Since both races must know that the contents and flavour of brown and white eggs do not differ in any way, the preference can only be the result of some atavistic superstition.

There are other superstitions connected with boiled eggs, and one of them is an old French belief that eggs should be boiled in *bouillon*. Well, having tried this method in a strong bouillon made of meat stock cubes, I have to report that when the egg is cooked it doesn't taste of the bouillon and the bouillon doesn't taste of the egg.

However, boiling the bouillon does make a nice smell around the kitchen and a little of the smell sticks to the outside of the shell. But the egg itself is not affected. No doubt this will come as a relief to the vegetarian; it is hardly much comfort to the expectant gourmet and ambitious Coarse Cook.

Most of what needs to be said about poached eggs has already been said on p. 48.

Once an egg has been poached all that concerns the Coarse Cook (who, after all, is going to eat it) is how to dish it up so that the yolk doesn't spread all over the plate.

Nothing you ever put a poached egg on seems to be big enough. If you put it on toast the bread is cut from too small a loaf; if you put it on spinach (which, without a cheese sauce, makes the egg *demi-Florentine*), the spinach never covers a large enough area. The only really safe foundation for a poached egg is a generous nest or bed— nay, field—of mashed potato.

My earliest gastronomic memory of any kind is, in fact, of a poached egg on mashed potato. I ate it when I was about three years old and my father took me to Brighton for the day. It made such an unforgettable impression on me that to this day a poached egg on mashed potato is as unfailingly satisfying and exotic as it was on that first occasion.

For many years, when deprecating the standard of English public cookery, it has been fashionable to say that in France even in the most humble inn you can at least always get a good omelette. If you can't get a good omelette in England, even in some far-from-humble inns, it must be because English cooks have been brought up on such a number of curiously contradictory methods.

Most Coarse Cooks will remember from their early and not very successful experiments in omelette-making how helpful friends constantly offered tips on the only *real* way to make an omelette. These tips, peculiar to the English and imparted with all the air of giving away closely-guarded professional secrets, ranged from adding a teaspoonful, a dessertspoonful, a tablespoonful of water, to adding a teaspoonful, a dessertspoonful, a tablespoonful of milk.

'My earliest gastronomic experience. . . .'

When we followed these cunning bits of advice we found that they did nothing to help the omelette at all. The more water you added the greater the area of the pan the mixture covered and the less it tasted of egg, while the addition of any milk whatever made the whole thing extremely tough.

In the end, one learnt that a good omelette had nothing to do with the addition of any foreign liquid, but everything to do with getting the pan and a little butter really hot, but not burnt, before pouring in the egg; not trying to cook too big an omelette and just watching for the critical moment when your experience told you the omelette was done.

Unlike almost any other dish, an omelette is a highly personal affair as you can fill it with virtually anything you like to think of, from 'Am and Anchovies to Yams and Zucchini.

C

An omelette which I have never made myself, but which was often cooked in our kitchen years ago, is Omelette Silvana. It is named after an Italian singer from La Scala who once stayed with us, and it is the sort of omelette that might well be something for Coarse Cooks with Coarse Children who have (in Francatelli's sense) Coarse Appetites.

Silvana heated some olive oil in a frying pan and threw in a handful of cold potato, or cold cooked spaghetti, sometimes with chopped onion, carrots, tomatoes and anything that happened to have been left over from the previous meal.

When this mixture was hot the beaten eggs were added —enough eggs, it should be said, to fill a large pan to the depth of one inch. The omelette was then cooked until it was thoroughly set. It was then covered with a large meat plate, turned over and slid back in the pan and cooked until the other side was brown and solid.

Silvana then dished her omelette out on to a plate again and cut herself a triangular slice out of it, as though it were cake. What was left over was put away and eaten cold next time.

If you know how much singers have to eat to sing you will realise that it was a good nourishing body-building dish. Just the thing, in fact, for ravenous children, although, of course, they may insist on eating potato crisps with it.

There remains the question of scrambled eggs. If you consider that they should be cooked only in a double boiler, then that is when you make a show of modesty and helplessness and insist that you would not be so presumptuous as to trespass on your wife's territory.

However, since the invention of the non-stick saucepan, your wife may prefer to give the double boiler a miss, anyway, and encourage you to make your own scrambled eggs.

Rightly or wrongly, I have always made scrambled eggs in a frying pan with lots of butter, stirring them like mad with a wooden spoon, and taking the pan off the fire before they get too solid. Guests often remark on the unusual quality of my chunky omelettes, but so long as *I* know I've cooked scrambled eggs that is all that matters.

Artists are used to being misunderstood.

FISH

With static and mobile fried fish shops around so many corners, the cooking of fish in batter and deep fat is one thing the Coarse Cook need not worry about—unless, that is, he is so dead set on eating whitebait that he considers all the deep-fry paraphernalia is worth while.

It is the nature of the average Coarse Cook, however, to avoid elaborate and messy cooking whenever possible. Some may consider that this must limit his repertoire in the case of fish. Well, it may limit it; but think of the class of fish you're limiting it to. Cooking a live lobster involves no more than dropping it into a pan of sea-water (or salted fresh water) and making a good mayonnaise to go with it, caviar no more than opening a jar and cutting a few wedges of lemon.

The cookery of oysters, on the other hand, can get a little too fanciful. I have an old English cookery book which lists no fewer than thirty different ways of being careless with oysters. They include oysters in batter, boiled, grilled, fried, fricassé'd, made into fritters, ketchup and sausages, minced, pickled, and cooked on skewers with mushrooms and bacon like shashlik.

One of the easiest oyster recipes in the book is called, for a reason the author doesn't explain, Mouth Soup:

> Make a rich mutton broth, with two large onions, three blades of mace, and black pepper. Strain it and pour it on a hundred and fifty oysters, previously bearded, and a bit of butter, rolled in flour. Let it simmer gently a quarter of an hour, and then serve.

Come the Revolution, we might try it sometime.

For the Coarse Cook who wants to get on with the cooking and enjoy quick results there is nothing to beat trout or sole *à la meunière* for ease of execution and gastronomic class.

All you need is a frying pan with hot butter in it, fish that has been lightly 'dusted' (how's that for dainty cooking talk?) with a very little flour, and about fifteen or twenty minutes to fry the fish gently on both sides.

When they're done, you put the fish on to a dish, melt some more butter which you pour over them when it is frothy, and add chopped parsley and lots of lemon juice.

If you grow sick of trout and sole you can always cook herrings and mackerel *à la meunière*, but it is not recommended for the queasy. It makes the rich fish richer and the poorly feel poorlier.

Or, as a change, you can try an extremely simple recipe for boiled trout, *truite Mme Beeton*. You simmer a couple of medium-sized trout for ten to twelve minutes and when they're done serve them with a sauce of one-third of a pint of melted butter with a tablespoonful of coarsely chopped gherkin in it.

Perhaps Mme Beeton's method may not be as glamorous as trout *meunière*, but at least it is five or ten minutes quicker. And the washing up isn't such a business.

For less urgent occasions fish poached in dry white wine or cider is a very straightforward and satisfactory method which doesn't leave the kitchen smelling too strongly of fish for days afterwards. (I know I suggested earlier that poaching fish was a little too *haute* for Coarse Cookery, and that once you started doing it you had your foot on the bottom rung of the wrong ladder. But there is no harm in acting *haute* from time to time, provided you don't advertise it too blatantly.)

Poaching in wine does, however, sometimes produce a rather marked and evocative atmosphere of fermentation, such as you get in a cellar full of wine casks. This is because in his discovery of the joys and possibilities of cooking with wine, the Coarse Cook is inclined to let his enthusiasm run away with him.

And why not? It has been a well-known fact, and loudly proclaimed for centuries by gastrologers, that cooking with wine aids the digestion. What, then, more logical and natural for the Coarse Cook, whose digestion inevitably suffers in the early stages of his career, than to cook with wine and plenty of it?

There comes a time, however, when the *digestif* itself becomes a dyspeptic agent and the Coarse Cook, understandably puzzled by this sudden denial of all he has been brought up to believe, in desperation turns to his reference books for help. What he finds is unexpected and disillusioning: the poaching is done with water—enough to cover the fish in its pan, and a glass of wine is merely added.

It doesn't take any qualified Coarse Cook long to recognise that this is an obvious mistake, the result of an universally committed editorial error. The quantities and ingredients have been reversed: for water, read wine; for wine, read water. So instead of cooking only in wine as before, he uses just enough wine to cover the fish and adds a glass of water. This keeps the question of dilution in its proper perspective and will most certainly restore the famous digestive properties of wine used in cookery.

The use of white wine in poaching fish is of considerable 'invisible' economic importance. Unless a lot of it is used in cooking, the Balkan countries who sell their white wine to us will not have enough currency to buy British motor cars and lavender water in return. There is no other way I know of using up this sort of wine; it is too acid to drink.

Suggested fish to poach with wine and fresh herbs (sprigs of tarragon, parsley, fennel and thyme): cod fillets, plaice, turbot, halibut and salmon trout.

MEAT

I am tied to the steak and must stand the course
SHAKESPEARE

 I don't know whether the character who spoke those words (more or less) in *King Lear* was speaking for the people of Ancient Britain, but he was certainly speaking for the people of England today.

There may have been a time when the roast beef of Old England was, in fact, the national dish and, we are assured by British travel advertising, is still served at every meal in the surroundings of a perpetual Dickensian Christmas. Today, however, a generation is growing up with a quite remarkable appetite for steaks and virtually no other form of meat—the result one imagines of being war babies of deprived parents who suffered years of severe rationing. If that is the reason, it is a generation which is making up for lost time in no half-hearted manner.

Although naturally Coarse Cookery includes grilling among its processes and practices (the subject was discussed fully on pp. 32–5), the fact that there are probably millions of ravenous young carnivores who can grill their supper does not automatically entitle them to rate as Coarse Cooks, unless they can do something else. We do not encourage one-dish cookery in our ranks if we can help it.

The 'O' level of meat cookery demands proficiency in at least two methods; the 'A' level, three or more. Methods that produce the most immediate results are naturally the most popular, and the majority of those with 'O' levels have qualified with grilling and frying. Some people consider that frying sausages shouldn't count, but they are reminded that the Boy Scout's cooking of sausages is one of the rocks on which Coarse Cookery is founded. As well say that frying an egg 'doesn't count'.

The frying of meat may sound a little primitive and

even proletarian; nevertheless, it is a process which can result in far from primitive and proletarian dishes. You can't make a Wiener Schnitzel, for instance, without a frying pan; or a sole *meunière*. The Coarse Cook, however, who isn't running a caff and therefore has no need to deceive anyone but himself (and he is too experienced to do that), finds the genuine Wiener Schnitzel just the sort of thing which presents no technical problems but, when finished, looks as if it had come from Frau Sacher's restaurant itself.

When you have beaten your thinly sliced fillets of veal with a mallet or milk bottle, moisten them on both sides with wine vinegar. This is not the conventional way to begin a Wiener Schnitzel, but it was a tip given to me by a senior Coarse Cook during my apprenticeship many years ago. At that time I shared a house on the Thames Embankment (Tate Gallery end) with a number of medical students, and Wiener Schnitzel was a recurrent item on the menu. It was the only thing I knew how to cook at that time, and it made a change from kippers, which was the only thing anybody else knew how to cook. Supplies of veal and a large block of ice were delivered every day by a large West End store where somebody's aunt had an account she unwisely permitted her nephew to use.

The ice, of course, was because the refrigerator was not in general use among the penniless young and veal was likely to go off.

It has not occurred to me until now that the brushing of veal fillets with vinegar for Schnitzels may possibly have been recommended by our well-wisher because one lot of veal I was preparing had begun to go off, and the vinegar would revive, or at least disguise, it. Yes, quite likely that was it.

At any rate, I have dutifully vinegared my Wiener Schnitzel ever since in the belief that it gave the meat a subtle piquancy. It can be confidently recommended.

After this initial ritual the fillets are dipped in beaten egg, coated with breadcrumbs and sauté'd on each side in the ordinary way.

Then comes the garnishing.

Although I am sure there are strict rules in High Cookery about what garnish you add to what dish, in Coarse Cookery complete freedom of self-expression is part of our birthright, and decorative and original garnishes are encouraged at all times. The subject of garnishes is discussed more fully in a later section.

The pure, classic Wiener Schnitzel is said by some to be garnished only with slices of lemon. We are not purists or classicists, so when we garnish we do so with imagination and a liberal hand.

'. . . when we garnish we do so with imagination
and a liberal hand.'

Slices of lemon? Granted; but they are peeled and one slice is placed on each fillet with a stoned green olive. Decoration with edibility is the principle of our Schnitzel garnish, therefore a generous number of anchovy fillets are artistically arranged in stripes or crosses on the fillets with, of course, capers. No anchovies without capers is a time-honoured slogan in Coarse Cuisine. And where there are anchovies there must also be eggs. Each fillet is garnished with a neat little heap of the chopped white, and another of the chopped yolk, of hard-boiled eggs.

Some operators prefer to put the egg garnish on the side of the plate instead of on the veal, but to the majority of consumer-cooks half the fun of this particular dish is getting as much garnish on top of the meat as possible, so that each mouthful of Schnitzel includes a noticeable proportion of garnish.

The garnish can be further elaborated by the addition of black olives, finely sliced sweet gherkin and a pinch of chopped chives on top of the chopped egg.

There is no earthly need to stone the olives, either green or black. We're not cooking for people who are too refined to spit the stones out on to their plates, as they do when they eat a Salade Niçoise. Stoned olives is carrying gracious living too far.

Garnish is also an important feature of Steack Tartare (I prefer the French spelling for a dish which is more expertly presented in France). No cooking is involved, of course, but a certain amount of careful preparation is needed. Ideally, the steak should be fillet and scraped by hand, so that none of the blood is lost as it is by mincing. For most of us, however, it is a question of buttock steak and mincing, having neither the money for fillet nor the patience for scraping.

A good Steack Tartare starts out looking as pretty as a picture—the raw egg-yolk sitting in the middle of its nest of meat, the finely chopped parsley, shallot or garlic (some like both) sprinkled over it with perhaps a shake of paprika and a couple of anchovy fillets added. It ends up a glorious appetising mash, enriched by the olive oil the consumer adds to it according to his taste.

This is the Coarse Cook's classic way of making a Steack Tartare.

The great thing to be remembered is that it is a dual-purpose dish, like one of those reversible coats that are tweed one side and mackintosh the other. If you are suddenly faced with a guest who doesn't like raw meat, all you need do is cook it in a frying pan with a little olive oil, or better still, on a griddle without any. You can then—in the manner of those London caffs who talk of 'beef-burgers' in the belief that hamburgers must be made of ham—call the result a *steack fille-de-joie*, or tartburger.

POULTRY AND GAME

. . . Heigh! the sweet birds
SHAKESPEARE

 This is a branch of cookery the Coarse Cook is not usually very familiar with. It is, to be frank, a bit of a business. It isn't like meat, which you can cook in a couple of ways all your life and still get the maximum enjoyment out of. Grilling and roasting meat involve you in comparatively little in the way of frilly extras and garnishes. Even with roast lamb one can get away with red currant or mint jelly out of a jar if it's a trouble to make a fresh mint sauce.

But think of what you have to provide with chicken, duck, pheasant, turkey, goose, quail, snipe, grouse, part-ridge and the rest, once you start—bread sauce, game chips, orange salad, fried breadcrumbs, stuffing, toast, cranberry sauce, and heaven knows how many sauces made with giblets, port, Marsala and Burgundy. The cooking of coot can even entail making a cup of drinking chocolate to be poured over it in order to disguise the bird's strong flavour of fish. Or so a French recipe insists.

This is no corner of the cooking field for the Coarse Cook to bother himself with. He soon discovers that the best sort of poultry for his temperament and talent is grilled spring chicken. It involves no sauces or lengthy cooking; it is a clean, simple, direct approach to a subject which is otherwise messy, elaborate and time-consuming.

Unfortunately, ever since we were landed with that New and Improved gas cooker with its useless grill I have personally been unable to enjoy this particular form of Coarse Cookery. As any other way of cooking poultry, let alone game, demands more skill than my status in the kitchen allows, I might count myself deprived and under-privileged were it not that I live with a cook who can even jug a hare if need be.

But she doesn't do it often, unfortunately. It's the repulsive look of the raw ingredients that she objects to and which keeps game off our menus, rather than any shortage of raw material. Our estate (1348·63 square metres) is full of game—belonging to other people, whose pheasants, pigeons and partridges, hares and rabbits, treat the garden like a hotel. Now and then, when we consider they are abusing the hospitality of our game reserve, we take punitive measures, though not with much success. So far our bag is one small rabbit confiscated from our cat. This was done for the cat's health, when he was suffering from too much protein in his diet. The result was a good *lapereau en casserole*.

An attempt to shoot a pheasant with a catapult, on the other hand, had a happy ending—for the pheasant. I fired the pebble straight into the thumb of my left hand which was holding the catapult. It took nearly two years for the black of the bruised thumbnail to grow out.

However, there is never any shortage of pheasant in our part of the country, and therefore no need for the Coarse Cook to feel he is missing anything by not in-cluding it in his repertoire. Since the invention of the deep freeze one is constantly asked out to dinner in the summer by hosts desperate for guests to help them eat up the scores of pheasants that have been stored away since the end of the previous season.

VEGETABLES

 Although there is little that is basically very complicated about this branch of Coarse Cookery it is nevertheless a very tricky one. It involves timing and it involves the control of heat—two aspects of cooking which can be acquired only by experience and experiment, by frustrating trial and ghastly error.

The main trouble is that by the time you come to cook something a little more imaginative than boiled potatoes, you are too old to have access to advice. Or if you are given advice, you are still too inexperienced to put it into successful practice.

There was that business about *petits pois à la française*, for instance. A kind friend in a pub told me how to do it: I was to place a couple of wet lettuce leaves in the bottom of a saucepan and put in the peas on top of them. Then I was to add salt, a good knob of butter and sprinkle half a teaspoonful of sugar into the pan. The water in the lettuce would be enough to cook the peas, my friend assured me. It was the classic French method and would take twenty minutes.

I did as I was told, turned the gas up to the usual height needed to boil eggs and potatoes or anything else, and went to play the piano to pass the time.

After twenty minutes I went back to the kitchen to put the peas on one side while I cooked my nightly Wiener Schnitzel, prepared, of course, in advance.

The peas came out as exquisite *petits pois en forme de balles à la française*—tiny black bullets made of iron which would have served admirably as lethal ammunition for a peashooter. It was not at all what I had expected.

When I told my kind friend in the pub what had happened, he accepted no responsibility. He had never actually cooked peas that way, or any other way; his wife did all the cooking and he had overheard her telling a friend how *petits pois à la française* were done. So we went and asked his wife about it, and it was then that I first heard of putting a lid on the saucepan and cooking the peas on a very low flame. How could one ever have known about that?

A much easier way of cooking peas is one which, since it hasn't got a name, we can christen *petits pois à la brésilienne*. Instead of boiling a packet of frozen peas in water, you boil them in slightly sweetened black coffee. The peas absorb the flavour of the coffee in whatever time the packet says they should be boiled, and the result is unusual and pleasant.

The peas lose their emerald-green colour, of course, acquiring instead the kind of black-and-tan South American Indian complexion found in Brazil, the place there's an awful lot of coffee in.

One of the principal bores of vegetable cooking has always been the preparation of vegetables. By definition the Coarse Cook does not have a Coarse Scullery Maid to do all the peeling and scraping and removal of insects. He has to do that himself.

The really conscientious Coarse Cook will not be deterred from cooking the vegetable he fancies merely because its preparation is irksome. There are some, however, who prefer to take a line of virtually no resistance, like one Coarse Cook I know who will never cook potatoes that have to be peeled. As his religion forbids him to use instant mashed potato, he just bakes potatoes in their jackets whenever there are no new potatoes in season that can be boiled after a light scrubbing.

When he cooks new potatoes he naturally adds a sprig or two of mint. This is a purely ritual gesture, to make the kitchen smell good, he says. The quickest way of making mint tasteless is to put it into boiling water with new potatoes. The time to add mint, he insists, is when the potatoes are done and you are putting butter on them before serving.

With a pair of scissors he cuts fresh raw mint into small pieces over the potatoes. All the bedraggled leaves of

boiled mint are thrown away or left in the saucepan that
robbed them of their flavour.

There are other Coarse Cooks, too, who never eat
onions at home because of the painful effects of peeling
and slicing or chopping them up. But the shedding of
tears is not an indispensable feature of onion preparation.

In my early Wiener Schnitzel days I heard that if
onions were sliced under water they wouldn't make your
eyes water. As the kitchen sink was usually full of pot
plants when I wanted to slice onions, I ran my bath and
cut them up in that. Before getting into the bath I scooped
out the onion, which floated on the surface, with a colander,
or a frying basket, and transferred it to a washbasin full
of water to stay there until it was wanted.

When the onion was to be cooked it was put in a frying
pan with a couple of spoonfuls of olive oil, covered with a
large plate, or the breadboard, and fried very slowly
over a low flame. When they were done the onions were
delicious, the nearest thing, we always considered, to the
wonderful onions frying in the window of Harris's cab-
men's sausage restaurant in Whitcomb Street, off Leicester
Square (with a branch in West Street, Brighton, also
long gone).

The frying pan used with a gentle touch on the stove
solves many of the problems of vegetable cookery, and
heaven knows there are plenty of these problems in the
Coarse Kitchen.

I have a West Indian friend, a musician of great talent
and versatility, who, many years ago, used to receive food
parcels from home containing sweet potatoes, yams,
bread fruit, egg plants, and a varied selection of exotic
root vegetables looking like turnips and swedes, and all
twice as hard. I was regularly given an enormous bagful
of these things to take home—many of them, I have since
discovered, coming from either the same botanical order
as the deadly nightshade, or the convolvulus.

The donor had no views on how all this material should
be cooked, so I treated the whole lot like onion: stewed
them very slowly in oil with the pan covered.

The unexpectedly edible dish that resulted was offered to guests as a *maqu'-à-patouille* (say it 'muck-up-a-too-ee') *Christophe Colombe*.

The traditional *ratatouille* from which the West Indian stew and its name are distantly derived is, of course, an absolute natural for all Coarse Cooks. All you need is a covered pan and some olive oil, and winter and summer you have a highly foreign, but simple, dish that can be eaten hot or cold.

According to the season you can make our sort of ratatouille with aubergines, courgettes, red, green or yellow pimentos, tomatoes, onions, celery, leeks, lots of garlic—in fact, almost anything you fancy except parsnips.

Parsnips, famous in legend as the vegetable fine words won't butter, are believed by the English to produce delirium and madness when they are old (the parsnips, that is). The French sometimes credit them with aphrodisiac qualities. They say the same about celery and oysters.

The myth about oysters dies hard. Surely by now everybody knows that the true aphrodisiac is not the oysters, or even the Guinness, but the brown bread and butter that goes with them.

'. . . the brown bread and butter that goes with them.'

SALADS

You can make a salad with anything except washed lettuce that hasn't been dried, tomatoes that haven't been peeled, cucumber that hasn't been drained, and salad cream out of a bottle.

If you want an easy dressing, try this one which has impeccable origins, but has been successfully used by three generations of Coarse Cooks in our family and is called Clementina Cunliffe's Dressing.

Ingredients: Two hard-boiled egg-yolks
One tablespoonful of wine vinegar
Salt and freshly ground black pepper
A teaspoonful of made English mustard
Single cream

Mash the egg-yolks with a fork until they're quite smooth. Add the salt, pepper, mustard and vinegar. Stir in enough cream to make the dressing the consistency you like.

And to save you going to look it up anywhere else, a recipe for a French or vinaigrette dressing:

Half a teaspoonful of salt
A quarter of a teaspoonful of dry English mustard
A good shake of freshly ground black pepper
Two overflowing (over-spilt?) tablespoonfuls of good olive oil

(By good olive oil, I mean not over-refined chemists' oil, but proper French, Spanish or Italian oil that tastes of something. We're eating it, not using it on babies' bottoms.)

One or two teaspoonfuls of wine vinegar, or wine vinegar mixed with lemon juice
A clove of garlic cut in two, if you're using it to rub round the bowl; or crushed if you aren't and prefer to eat it

A tablespoonful (or more) of mixed chopped fresh herbs—parsley, tarragon, chives, chervil

Put the salt, pepper, mustard powder, vinegar and chopped garlic into the salad bowl. Mix them up, then add the oil in a gentle trickle, stirring all the time until it is thoroughly blended.

Add the lettuce, sprinkle the herbs on top, and tire the lot out—or whatever the English is for *fatiguez*.

PUDDINGS

Puddings is/are a very personal subject for any Coarse Cook. Even more than poultry and game they are a business. Worse than that: for an astonishing number of Coarse Cooks puddings are something they personally never eat at all, but find themselves having to cook for guests who do.

The Coarse Cook who happens to like puddings, and considers them worth the trouble, will have learnt all he wants to know about them before he opens this book—even if it is only opening a tin of lichees and a carton of cream.

For the Coarse Cook who likes puddings I fear this section is not likely to prove very encouraging, and certainly not authoritative or instructive, for puddings is a branch of Coarse Cookery of which I have no experience whatever. The best I can do, therefore, is to pass on a recipe by a sweet-toothed friend which is less a matter of cookery than of lavish confection.

It is a chocolate pudding called Snuff Box, which consists of grated bitter chocolate mixed with rum on to which you put a layer of lightly whipped unsweetened cream; then a layer of chocolate; another of cream; another of chocolate; and so on.

My sweet-toothed friend, an enthusiast if ever there was one in the Coarse Kitchen, unfortunately neglects to say how much of the three ingredients is needed—largely, I

D

imagine, because he doesn't know. It is a matter of individual taste, he says, recalling that on the last occasion he put in three times the required amount of rum, with remarkable effect on the behaviour of his guests.

What the 'required amount' of rum can be is obviously anybody's guess. There is no doubt, however, that the 70 proof of this pudding is in the eating.

CHEESE

I'd rather live with cheese and garlic
SHAKESPEARE

This is the one course on the menu at which any Coarse Cook can shine. It is not only easy to produce, but can be a genuine *pièce de résistance*—for though in its strictest sense the phrase in French means a large joint of meat which is the centre-piece of a meal, it can also mean any dish substantial enough to perform the same function. An imaginatively conceived and arranged selection of cheeses can do this to perfection.

The cosmopolitan taste in food which has developed in England since the war has spread particularly to the cheese board. But not always with happy results. Too many imported cheeses are sold in this country when they are out of season.

Few people realise, for instance, that the season for Camembert is from October to June; and yet in England one is offered this cheese before it is ripe, or ever likely to ripen, or when it is so old that it stinks to high heaven. A French woman we knew, housekeeping for her husband while he sang at our local opera house, was horrified by the putrid condition of the first and only Camembert she has ever bought in England. She opened it when she got it home and had to bury it in the garden straight away; dustbins are emptied only once a fortnight hereabouts.

Brie is another queer one. If it comes from Meaux (Seine-et-Marne) it is best eaten from November to May;

if it comes from Melun (Seine-et-Marne), thirty-five miles away, the season is from October to June.

When one studies even the most familiar cheeses nearly all of them have their peak periods—Livarot from October to July, Pont-l'Évêque from October to June, Reblochon from September to July, Tomme au marc (with the grape pips) from November to May.

The habit, rapidly becoming international, of 'processing' may well alter all this to make all cheese uniformly harmless and tasteless all the year round. What little 'processed' French cheese I have been brave enough to taste so far has been remarkably characterless; if you want stinky cheese nowadays you cannot beat (or eat) the wrapped dark-blue squashy supermarket 'blue cheese'. It is sometimes so fierce that it cannot even be used for Pâté Clarence (see p. 55); it kills the Worcestershire sauce stone dead.

As the years have passed I must confess foreign cheeses are put out on the table only when there are guests; they seem to expect it. Or so we think, because that's what they do when we visit *them*.

If the truth were known, they probably behave when they're alone as we do: eat only English cheese. Things like red and blue Cheshire, Cheddar, Double Gloucester, Leicester, Derby, Cottenham, Wensleydale, Lancashire, carefully chosen Stilton, and Welsh Caerphilly (pronounced, foreign readers please note, 'Carfilthly' as in Llanelly), have become, I believe, the true connoisseur's cheeses. French cheese should be eaten in France, Italian cheese in Italy (particularly the soft table Parmesan); they taste better in their native air, and the best of them never reach England.

One should really be more courageous about this, and tell one's guests quite honestly that one considers imported cheese does neither credit to its makers nor honour to one's guests. In that way the whole pattern of present-day cheese-eating could well be changed for the better.

The only trouble, unfortunately, is that to suggest that English cheese is what tastes better in England may be regarded as jingoism or gastronomic ignorance. But that is a risk I imagine most Coarse Cooks will face with equanimity once they realise its truth.

SAVOURIES

The gradual disappearance of the after-dinner savoury from English life is mourned by few so much as by the Coarse Cook. Not because he wants the opportunity to produce savouries for his guests, but because he is rarely offered them nowadays when he dines out in polished-table-and-candles private houses.

It was there, he recalls sadly, that there were always Angels on Horseback, Devils on Horseback, Anchovy Eggs, Devilled Chickens' Livers, Baked Herring Roes, Marrow Toast, Roes on Toast, Foie Gras Toast, Scotch Woodcock, Curried Shrimps, Stuffed Tomatoes, Welsh Rabbit, Cheese Straws, Cheese Soufflés, or Mushrooms on Toast.

And today? What he used to expect as a *bonne bouche* is now often inflated into a main dish at many people's tables.

For the Coarse Cook who considers it is time a few of the standards to which he was educated were restored, and that if he doesn't do something about it, nobody else will, the classic books of English cookery are full of unexpected ideas for savouries.

Two of the most interesting are variants of the Welsh Rabbit (*not* 'rarebit', if you please—it is a joke dish, like Toad-in-the-Hole). The first is called Irish Rabbit, and it starts off like Welsh Rabbit—by melting the cheese in a saucepan with butter and beer. When this is creamy you add vinegar, made English mustard, pepper and finally some coarsely chopped gherkins. The mixture is poured on to hot well-buttered toast.

The other form is known as Yorkshire Rabbit. Again you melt the cheese in a saucepan with butter and beer, pepper and a little made mustard, but this time you add a few drops of Worcestershire sauce instead of vinegar. Meanwhile, you make a piece of well-buttered toast and poach two eggs in as tidily plump a form as possible. The cheese mixture is poured over the toast and the eggs are placed on top.

I suggested that the Coarse Cook might like to revive the custom of eating savouries, but if he shies a little at the idea of signing-off a meal with Yorkshire Rabbit, that is understandable. But there is nothing to prevent him making a meal of it when he is really ravenous.

In addition to the use of herbs and spices in the classic savouries, the invention of entirely new savouries which clearly conform to the traditional idea of the purpose and character of the dish also has many possibilities.

My only personal experience of this so far I have to admit has been a failure. I set out to produce a savoury which combined the features of two well-known recipes, and which I called Welsh Woodcock, or Scotch Rabbit. From the Welsh Rabbit I took the melted cheese, from the Scotch Woodcock the anchovy fillets and capers which decorate the buttered eggs in modern versions of this celebrated savoury; from both I took the hot buttered toast.

My invention, which in theory promised so well, was a failure because the anchovy and capers just didn't go with the cheese. It was most disappointing and I cannot work out what chemical reason there was for it. Perhaps one should mix the buttered eggs and melted cheese (with white wine) together and sprinkle capers over it. Anyway, the result was a dish which, if not insipid, was— to use the language of Professor Pelham Grenville Wodehouse—far from sipid.

But why stop at mixing only two savouries, I say. The English, with their remarkable appetites, could cope easily with features of the Yorkshire Rabbit as well. At least, I can't see any hungry teenager refusing a piece of toast piled high with the cheese-and-scrambled-egg mixture of the Celtic Wood-rabbit and topped with two plump poached eggs from Yorkshire.

SAUCES

 Sauces are always made by the sauce chef. If you do not have one in your kitchen, find one and marry her.

Or, if you prefer, and think it's less trouble, buy an electric mixer and learn to make a really good mayonnaise. It is not difficult, and earns you a tremendous reputation as a cook.

If your guests arrive while you are still making the mayonnaise, give them a drink and start on the well-known controversial subject of Mayonnaise: its History and Political Significance. This will pass the time pleasantly, airing a number of theories of varying degrees of preposterousness.

According to some gastrographers, the sauce was invented by the Duc de Richelieu (1696–1788) the day after, or the day before (they are not sure which), he captured Port Mahon, or Mahon, in Minorca in 1756 from the English who'd taken it from the Spanish forty-four years before. To celebrate the occasion the Marshal named the sauce Mahonnaise. Who corrupted it to mayonnaise, why, and when, nobody is prepared to say.

Another lot of gastrographers deny that the sauce has anything to do with Mahon. How, they ask, could a busy Marshal like Richelieu have had time to mess around with eggs and olive oil in the middle of fighting the English? Much more likely, they maintain, that the sauce was invented at Bayonne and that its correct name is 'bayonnaise'.

That may satisfy some people, but it doesn't explain how 'bayonnaise' could conceivably become 'mayonnaise'. The corruption can only have happened the other way round—the result of somebody with a terrible code in the dose trying to say 'mayonnaise'.

As for the theory that mayonnaise originally came from a place called Mayonne, this might wash if anybody could tell us where Mayonne might be; but they can't.

After studying all the evidence there is only one con-

'. . . find one and marry her.'

clusion to be reached: somebody wanted to give a name
to a delicious sauce of egg-yolk and olive oil so they called
it mayonnaise.

Whatever else could they possibly call it?

GARNISHES

 A garnish, in English public eating, is the
soggy chips, tinned peas and half-grilled
half-tomato that you didn't ask for, which
are always served with your grilled steak.
Fortunately, what English 'restauranteurs'
(as they now miscall themselves) consider
a garnish, and why, is nothing to do with us, for the
term means something quite different in the Coarse
Kitchen.

To us, the garnish (as I have already said) is the final,
supreme means of culinary self-expression, for there is no
limit to what you can invent, or try out, in the way of
fantastic combinations of flavours, colours, fruit, vegetable,
fish, meat, spices, herbs, ranging from the simple sprig of
watercress needed for a steak to the quenelles, cockscombs,
cock's kidneys, truffles, mushrooms and stoned olives of a
garniture Financière.

It is mostly among the garnishes that you encounter
the things that do more than just taste good. Anthelme
Brillat-Savarin (1755–1826), born at Belley (where
better?), is the most often-quoted and least-read of all
food reporters, and his typical purple-patch-prose over-
writing has incurably infected the literature of food and
wine to this day. He once described the truffle as the
diamond of cookery.

Dumas, for his part, claimed that the truffle arouses
'erotic and gourmand memories in the sex that wears
dresses' (he means women), 'and gourmand and erotic
memories in the sex that wears beards' (he means men).

'The truffle,' continued Dumas, 'is not a positive
aphrodisiac, but on occasion it can make women more
loving and men more lovable.' This is highly probable
with truffles now costing as much as an emerald necklace.

After all, what girl with a cultivated taste is not an expert snapper-up of carefully considered truffles?

Dumas, whose observations on the qualities of truffles we have just noted, was, of course, a literary figure of some distinction. So, too, was Edward Lear, who gave considerable thought to food, even listing the diet of the Owl and the Pussy-cat which consisted, apart from honey, of mince and slices of quince—a good example of an unusual garnish.

Unlike Dumas, however, Lear did not leave us any recipes and there is no hint anywhere in his *œuvre* (which is modern English for the French phrase, *son output*) of how to prepare his garnish of those Chocolate Shrimps from the Mill, which he used to buy with pancakes and lotion.

Research, however, suggests that reference to the Mill is a pun, and that the chocolate to be used is the famous bitter Chocolat Menier, which Lear distorts into 'Meunier', or Miller's Chocolate. One looks in vain for what in High Cookery would surely be known as *Crevettes chocolat à la mode du moulin*.

In spite of my admiration of Edward Lear, however, I think this is probably a rather overrated garnish.

For those who grow them in their gardens, nasturtium seeds can be quite simply pickled to make an unusual garnish of what are sometimes called 'English capers'. All you need is another of those large jars of pickled dill cucumbers. Eat, or give away, all the cucumbers as before, and in the liquor that remains put a couple of good handfuls of young nasturtium seeds picked when they are about the size of *petits pois* very *fins*.

Close the jar tightly and leave it for two or three months, when the nasturtium seeds will be soft and fit to eat. They won't ever taste like real capers, but they'll look rather like them, and they taste surprisingly well.

Another method of pickling nasturtium seeds is to pick them when they are fully grown, boil them in wine vinegar for an hour and bottle in the vinegar when it is cold. Wait two or three months before opening the jar, when the seeds will be as hard as ball bearings and quite

D*

inedible. They will also be inedible if you wait for six months. Or a year. Or five years.

Real capers—the seeds of the *capperis spinosa* of southern Europe—are not only a delicious garnish that goes with everything, but an inseparable element in the most useful garnish of all: anchovy fillets and capers.

If capers by themselves go with everything, anchovy fillets and capers go twice as well with everything. It is an all-purpose garnish without parallel in Coarse Cookery.

If you have nothing to garnish, or even nothing to eat, you need never starve so long as you have anchovy fillets and capers. And you can't say that about any old garnish, can you?

FOREIGN COOKERY

Frogs and snails and puppy-dogs' tails
ANTI-COMMON MARKET MARCHING SONG

The English have enjoyed public eating of foreign foods of all kinds for many generations now, but it is only comparatively recently that the habit of trying to cook foreign food to be consumed on the premises has spread to the Coarse Kitchen.

My unsuccessful attempt to cook *petits pois à la française*, which I have already described, was made at a period when domestic cooking of this kind—whether it came off or not—was regarded as novel and a little exotic, if not actually *avant-garde*.

But today there are thousands of Coarse Cooks up and down the country whose kitchens are filled with the acrid smoke of what would have been *petits pois à la française*, if only they'd known about cooking with a low flame and the lid on.

The easiest introduction to foreign cookery is through those dishes classically described as *à l'anglaise*:

Broad beans boiled with savory and served with fresh butter are *fèves à l'anglaise*;
French beans served with butter are *haricots verts à*

l'anglaise (in England, of course, they appear on the
menu as being *au beurre*);
Potatoes *à l'anglaise* are shaped, cooked in a steamer
(which is an obvious anachronism, as chips have been
potatoes *à l'anglaise par excellence* for years now).

An old English cookery book, on the other hand, tells
us that potatoes *à l'anglaise* are boiled until they are nearly
done, when they are cut into slices and lightly fried in
butter. They are seasoned with salt, pepper and nutmeg.
This is a pretty foreign dish too, I'd say.

What is called *foie à l'anglaise* shows the French adopting
a much tidier treatment of liver and bacon than the
English. The liver is thinly sliced, grilled, and dressed
alternately with grilled rashers of bacon.

One of the most un-English dishes the French associate
with England is not literally classed as *à l'anglaise*. It is
ris de veau à la mode de Brighton—an uniquely English resort
with an uniquely exotic atmosphere. This is a dish of cold
braised sweetbreads, stuffed with tongue and truffles,
surrounded by artichoke hearts filled with vegetables in
mayonnaise, and garnished with chopped aspic. It'll be
a great day when Brighton gets to hear of this.

Finally, proving once and for all that one side of the English Channel doesn't know how the other side lives, the
French commend to us *huîtres à l'anglaise*. Obviously they
don't know that one of the happiest economic consequences
of the Welfare State is that the working classes no longer
have to eat oysters. They can now afford fish and chips. The
world of the author of *Les Aventures de M. Pickwick, La petite
Dorrit*, and *Les Contes de Noël* has long ago ceased to exist.

Oysters in the English manner, according to the French,
are not served raw and delicious to keen customers sitting
up at the bar of Bentley's or Wheeler's or English's, but
are set on a skewer with alternating pieces of bacon,
seasoned with cayenne, and grilled.

That sort of slanderous talk can do considerable
damage to an Entente that has never been over-Cordiale
at the best of times.

The first important lesson to learn in Italian cookery is to know how to tell good salami from poor ones before you buy them. Pinch them, and unless they're soft to finger and thumb leave them for other less cautious customers and go somewhere else.

The more ambitous student of *la cucina italiana* will, of course, want to progress quickly to the cooking of *pasta*. This can be very difficult for the English, as much of their childhood is spent with mums who make macaroni cheese. The English repertoire of macaroni dishes, indeed, is extensive and odd. If you are dead keen on macaroni that has been tampered with, Mrs Beeton has recipes for Macaroni and Cream (served on fried or toasted bread), Macaroni and Onion Fritters, Macaroni Pudding (with optional marmalade or raspberry jam), and Sweet Macaroni, which is cold, and covered with custard and grated nutmeg.

First attempts, on reaching the age of discretion, to break away from the English tradition and cook *pasta* in the unadorned Italian manner are rarely successful. The macaroni, spaghetti, tagliatelle, or whatever, come out of the saucepan of boiling water soft and sticky enough to paste up wallpaper with it, or so undercooked and hard that you can knit with it.

Presuming that you have learnt to put it into boiling salted water, knowing when the *pasta* is done comes only after experience and a lot of dropping of spaghetti off the fork and burning of tongues as you try to test its texture with your teeth.

Having decided that it's cooked as you like it, take it off the heat at once and quickly pour a tablespoonful of cold water into the saucepan. This isn't one of those mystical omelette-making tips we've heard about, but a means of preventing the *pasta* from cooking after the crucial moment of being just right.

This is a general habit among Italian cooks, and a practice learned from our friend, the inventor of the famous Omelette Silvana.

While we may consider the French idea of how food is

cooked *à l'anglaise* a little bizarre, it is only fair to say that
the English view of foreign cooking can be just as eccentric
in its own way. For me Omelette Silvana has always
been the ultimate Italian omelette; but not for the famous
early nineteenth-century cook Richard Dolby, of the
Thatched House Tavern in St James's.

His omelette *à l'italienne* is proposed in one long sentence:

> Break your eggs as usual, add salt, pepper, shred
> parsley, cream and olive oil; beat these ingredients well,
> and make three or four omelets of them, thin, but not
> too dry; cut some anchovies into thin slips, which lay
> on each of the omelets, placing the latter one on the
> other; cement them together, and when cold, having
> beaten up two eggs, dip in the omelets, bread and fry
> them to a nice colour.

Whether the 'omelets' are edible after passing through
two distinct cookery processes is another matter. But as
double-decker sandwiches made of egg instead of bread,
and fried to a nice colour, this dish might appeal as a foray
into the exotic to the more adventurous Coarse Cook;
though not, perhaps, to his guests.

Home Coarse Spanish Cookery is almost impossible in
England. This is because the peculiar brand of rancid olive
oil, produced in Spain by months of patient use and re-use
in the same paella pan, is unobtainable in this country.

INVALID COOKERY

In sickness and in health

There are two sorts of Invalid Cookery.

The first is what you have to cook for
yourself when your wife goes into hospital.

The second is what you have to cook
for your wife when she comes out of
hospital.

When your wife is in hospital you
revert, as everybody knows, to a bachelor
state—not merely in not having a woman about the house
to look after you, but in a rather carefree, not to say

costly, attitude to catering and general household management.

This is made all the easier because, as a senior and respected citizen, you now have accounts with all your tradesmen, and like all those who live alone, you can't be bothered to cook. You can't be bothered, that is, to cook anything but the most straightforward and untroublesome things—like grilled steaks and chops and veal cutlets, and slim fillets of veal that at any other time, when a washer-and-clearer-upper was around, you would make into a Wiener Schnitzel.

With nobody to disturb or inconvenience in the kitchen, I have found that this period of invalid cookery can be profitably spent in experimenting with the various 'media' of cookery, among them the charcoal grill.

I had better explain that the charcoal grill is the same contraption as the portable circular barbecue on three legs. It is called a charcoal grill indoors and a barbecue out of doors. The advantage of using the apparatus in the kitchen is that the charcoal is much easier to light if it is put in one of those spherical wire sieves used for shaking lettuce dry, and held over a gas flame until it is well alight and then transferred to the barbecue, where it is kept burning with the help of a pair of bellows or a Japanese fan.

The great joy of this method is that the smell, which out of doors is too often blown away by the wind, remains in the kitchen and adds noticeably to the general atmosphere of appetising cookery. And if it is still there at breakfast time, what better way of starting a new day anyway?

The second kind of Invalid Cookery is quite a different kettle of fish. The return of the lady of the house from hospital to convalesce brings with it a considerable adjustment of prices to incomes, and a certain amount of what is called re-thinking. The carefree days of grill-everything-and-to-hell-with-it are left behind, because if they were continued (it is gently pointed out) they would cost twice as much as before—if that was possible.

For households not equipped with an intercom or

walkie-talkie system, cookery for the convalescent invalid
involves the Coarse Cook in a great deal of running upstairs every five minutes or less, to consult his chef and
downstairs again to put her instructions into practice.
It is not that the invalid is having a meal cooked with
special care to suit her every whim; it is a question of
getting it cooked at all.

There is the business of basting the joint (after a fortnight of modern hospital food a girl needs something to
get her teeth into when she gets home), the demanding
operation of making gravy, the difficulty of trying to cook
the cabbage at the right time so that it coincides with the
potatoes so that the joint is cooked so that everything is
ready at the same moment.

Then there is the carving to be done; the knife hasn't
been used, let alone sharpened, during the weeks you have
been on a strict no-roast-joints régime. The plates and
vegetable dishes have to be warmed, the tray has to be
laid and finally taken upstairs. It is then found that there
is no salt, pepper or mustard on the tray, no napkins and
no serving spoons. These discoveries are made one after
another and each involves a journey down and up the
stairs.

However, considering the weight you put on during
your first period of Invalid Cookery the exercise you take
during the second can hardly do any harm.

Those who may think it tough on an invalid to be at the
mercy of a Coarse Cook during convalescence, don't know
how lucky modern invalids are.

In Mrs Beeton's family they ate a special Invalid Suet
Pudding, which differed from the normal Suet Pudding
only in being made with sugar and an egg and no baking
powder. It was served with honey, jam or golden syrup.

Not that there's any connection, but Mrs Beeton died
when she was twenty-nine.

HERBS

Better is a dinner of herbs where love is than a stalled ox and hatred
therewith
PROVERBS XV

AND SEASONING

You're the salt in my stew
TWENTIETH CENTURY LOVE SONG

 Because they are by nature adventurous
and given to experiments which those
who practise Higher Cookery are con-
vinced cannot succeed, Coarse Cooks
make the most imaginative use of herbs
and seasonings. This is especially the
case where they have gardens, for then
they have access to a remarkable variety of aromatic
plants which rarely, if ever, find their way into greengrocers' shops.

A well-stocked herb garden will contain chives and
Welsh onion, sage and thyme, rosemary and chervil,
marjoram and mint, basil and tarragon, garlic and
shallots, parsley, lemon thyme, fennel, lovage, bay leaves
and savory. And if they have gardens in the country their
choice is extended by the number of wild herbs to be found
in hedges and woods and on the hills. Wild marjoram,
wild thyme and the wild mints are subtle and desirable
variants of the tame garden species; and if you ever run
out of garlic, jack-by-the-hedge is a substitute that did us
well during the war, when garlic was unobtainable. I can
no longer remember what it looks like, so it is no good
telling you what to look for. In any case, with any luck,
we shan't be needing it again; next time France is
occupied we shall grow our own proper garlic (weather
permitting).

The many non-culinary uses of herbs and seasoning
plants are well known, of course. Rosemary can be
brewed into a hair-wash, for instance, and garlic is useful
in agoraphobia, or fear of crowds. Mustard baths cure

colds, and onion rubbed on the calf muscles prevents cramp.

The most versatile of all seasoning plants, however, is the juniper, whose berries are said to preserve the brain, strengthen the sight, clean the lungs, banish wind and facilitate digestion. A universal panacea, you might think —until you remember that juniper berries have only to be turned into gin for the brain to addle, the sight to weaken, the lungs to clog up, wind to rise and digestion to fail. It depends how it looks at you, really.

BARBECUES *or How To Get Pneumonia Using Only Three Matches*

Although for many of us the first experience of Coarse Cookery was out of doors as Boy Scouts, or Girl Guides, outdoor cooking is not something the average Coarse Cook shines at.

The preliminaries are all much too complicated for a start. Even with the elementary, foolproof, portable barbecue the difficulty of getting the charcoal to light, and having got it to light, of keeping it alight long enough to develop a glow hot enough to cook anything, is a hopelessly frustrating process. Attempts to light the charcoal with bits of paper which would light any normal fire result either in the paper smoking sullenly for a moment and going out, or burning so fast and fiercely that the flame has gone before the charcoal knows it.

Well-meaning friends hint that one should save up and buy an electrically operated barbecue. The hint is, of course, ignored as it is entirely contrary to the spirit of Coarse Cookery.

In the end there is nothing for it but to get the charcoal going over the gas in the salad drainer as before and take it outside, swinging it like a censer as you go, to keep it glowing.

The main disadvantage of a barbecue is that the very nature of the apparatus lets you in for luxury food. You can't make a stew on a barbecue, or boil an egg; even if you try liver and bacon the liver will grill nicely, but the bacon just evaporates the moment you lay a rasher on the grill.

So it has to be steaks and chops and veal cutlets as before; and to get the fire hot enough to grill them it takes you as much charcoal, time and trouble for two of you as it does for half a dozen or more.

Outdoor camp-fire-style cooking is something some clever people can manage successfully, but in my view it is even more difficult than the barbecue for the likes of us. Coarse Cookery must never be made difficult, or it ceases to be fun, and when it ceases to be fun it ceases to be Coarse Cookery. Personally, I have never been much of a one for camping and cooking in the open anyway. I tried once to cook a fish wrapped up in damp newspaper and put it to bake in the ashes, but the paper caused a lot of steam and the ashes just lay down and died. The fish never cooked, so I had to open a tin of something.

4

Ethics and Customs

Plat de la Nuit: A woman is a dish
SHAKESPEARE

Since the Art of Coarse Cookery is as old as Man himself,
it has a long tradition of laws, unwritten but instinctively
observed, of behaviour in the kitchen and at the dining
table, of etiquette and convention.

One of the oldest and most important is punctuality.
According to Brillat-Savarin 'the one thing indispensable
in a cook is punctuality; this applies to the guests also'—
which just shows the yawning gap between High and
Coarse Cookery. For us, the one thing indispensable is
punctuality—but only in a guest. The cook tries his best
to get everything done on time, but on the very rare
occasion when he does succeed it is essential for his self-
respect that his guests should be there at the off.

The choice of guest has also always been important.
You don't invite people who have cooks at home unless
you have had a thoroughly undistinguished meal there; in
which case, you invite them to show how the poor live,
and what freedom from the tyranny of a resident cook
can mean.

The ideal guest is one of your own kind—who knows
de trouble you seen, who can help in a crisis, and may
even arrive early to run up some pudding or other which
you feel you ought to give one of the evening's *invités*, but
aren't skilled enough to produce yourself.

The Guest Artist system is one of the oldest and most

fruitful features of Coarse Cookery. The practice of visiting other Coarse Kitchens to perform your own speciality touches on an important principle: the acceptance of applause and compliments with becoming modesty, and criticism with good grace.

A dish you know you have, in fact, invented yourself must not be claimed as an original creation. It is a 'discovery', the result of a pure accident, not of some virtuoso experiments of your own. You can give it a fancy name if you like—*suprême de volaille Hyde Park Corner*, say—but you must pass on the recipe to any of your colleagues who may ask for it. There is always a chance that when you next go to dinner with them they will have added some new ingredient to your original, and improved it no end.

In which case, you take *their* recipe home with you.

Not all inventions are successful, of course. But whereas those that come off are referred to as felicitous 'discoveries', those that don't may be credited to and blamed on whoever is your particular *bête noire* among the Fleet Street kitchen reporters. My own particular black beast (*bête* is feminine, you'll note) is one who refers to food being 'washed down' with wine—which is no way for anybody, let alone a lady, to talk or to drink.

If she were an educated Coarse Cook she would know, of course, that food is never washed down with anything. Dirty dishes are washed up. Only the draining board is washed down.

Whether cooking at home or away, it is an unshakeable tradition that the Coarse Cook should be served with bevers. A 'Bever' is an old English word for a drink drunk between meals.

To the Coarse Cook, who needs a series of large drinks to refresh him after cooking one meal, and a series of even larger ones to prepare him for cooking the next, a constant flow of bevers within easy reach of him in the kitchen is an absolute necessity.

The nature of these bevers is naturally a matter of personal taste. Some do well on Guinness, others on stiff dry martinis which have intriguing side-effects on the dishes, especially their garnishes and seasonings. Anything cooked in red wine, like kidneys, has a tendency to turn into red wine soup with kidneys floating in it. The fact that owing to one bever and another the dish you start out to cook turns into something quite different is of no importance. That is how brilliant and important discoveries are made in the Art of Coarse Cookery—and in Haute Cuisine too, if it were known.

Over the years it must be said that some of the more picturesque English customs have lapsed. There was a time, for instance, when at Christmas every gentleman sent a fat goose to the lady of the house he was in the habit of visiting. Beautiful women received a whole flock of them 'and were thus enabled to tell the number of their lovers by the number of fat geese sent to them'.

This custom was reported in a Paris newspaper of 1865, but indignantly denied by *The Times*. The French shrugged their shoulders and replied that there was no *fumée* without *feu*.

More unusual, however (this is purely parenthetic), was Tetrazzini's custom of giving a commemorative present of a watch to the various gentlemen of all classes and professions—but mostly waiters and taxi-drivers—who had shown her a good time and more.

When this story of the famous singer's generosity was told to the late Freddie Gaisberg, the H.M.V. impresario who first signed up Caruso to make records, he said, pointing to the grandfather clock behind him, 'I know. Tetrazzini gave me *that*.'

Naturally, like most Italian sopranos, Mme Tetrazzini could also cook.

COSTUME AND EQUIPMENT

This may seem a rather curious place to introduce a section one might reasonably expect to find at the very beginning of a cookery manual, but it is only after you have been cooking for some time that you begin to discover what you really need in the way of Costume and Equipment.

In an age when there is no limit to the style, cut and nature of the costume that can be worn on any occasion, when trouser-suits are accepted in the Royal Enclosure at Ascot, but not in some of the more royalist West End restaurants, what the Coarse Cook chooses to wear in the Coarse Kitchen is hardly affected by any traditions of precedents. The only tradition of Coarse Cookwear is that it should be comfortable and practical.

If you want to wear a tall white hat, a sweat rag, pale blue checked trousers and look a proper television Charlie, that is entirely your affair. And good luck to you, if you have a kitchen without a hood over the stove that knocks your hat off every time and is cool enough to make you want to keep your neckerchief on.

Most Coarse Cooks find that a one-piece head-to-toe asbestos suit, with built-in gloves, and worn with a mother's baby-bathing rubber apron, fireproof goggles and non-slip rubber boots, will ensure a certain amount of personal safety when engaged in basting joints or frying wet sliced potatoes.

Others, a little more reckless, but perhaps more agile, can manage to prepare a four-course meal dressed in no more than a bikini or a pair of running shorts. It is all a question of what makes you feel happiest in your work.

One thing is completely foreign to the spirit of Coarse Cookery, of course, and that is the sort of apron with facetious remarks embroidered on it, like 'His', 'Hers', 'Hooked at last!', 'You Wash—I'll Dry'. Unfortunately, very often these aprons are, in shape and size, exactly what you want, so much so indeed that there is nothing for it but to buy them and remove the soppy decoration from them at once.

The term Equipment in its general sense can cover everything a Coarse Cook needs in his armoury from an extractor fan to a salt spoon. In its particular sense, however, Equipment is what you haven't got when you most need it.

Everybody knows the typical lists of tools and gadgets

which the basic-cookery-books say are indispensable and
the absolute minimum needed if you are to cook so much
as a boiled egg. These inventories recommend (in addition to an initial supply of ten saucepans and four
frying pans) trussing needles, fancy vegetable cutters,
larding needles, cleavers, pestles, mortars, mincers,
colanders, sieves, chopping boards, pastry boards, conical
strainers, ordinary strainers, piping cornets, potato
mashers, porringers, scum strainers, graters, ladles,
wooden spoons, whisks, thermometers, rolling pins,
choppers, mixing bowls, pudding basins, fish and meat
flatteners, scissors, spatulas, egg slicers, vegetable scoops,
apple corers, potato peelers (left- and right-handed),
tin-openers, fish slices, tin funnels, ice-picks, marble
slabs, palette knives—everything except the really important things like nutcrackers for opening tightly screwed
bottle tops with, tongs for picking things up with, long
skewers for getting things out with, and extra flexible
scapulas for scraping up bits off the kitchen floor with.

There are, however, many utensils which still badly
need inventing to make Coarse Kitchen life easier.

One of them is a highly geared beater for those who
suffer from cream-whipper's wrist. The principle is
simplicity itself. The wheel you turn to operate the two
beaters is about eight inches in diameter, driving the
ordinary cog found on the normal, under-geared beater
at such speed that the driving wheel need be turned
scarcely more than a couple of times to beat any normal
egg to a frazzle. Patent not applied for, so anybody can
make a fortune out of my idea and good luck to them.

The mechanical, wheel-driven egg-beater is quite
contrary to classical cooking practice. When my wife was
being taught as a girl to cook, she was found to be beating
egg whites with a whisk, instead of a fork, and was
punished by having to make scones in her free time for a
week. The memory of this penalty has never faded, and
she beats egg whites with a fork to this day.

But as I was never at a domestic college, except the
one known as the Domestic College of Life—that is, the

Coarse Kitchen—I am waiting anxiously for somebody to market my high-gear, high-speed egg beater.

Another instrument that is needed is one for those of us who realise that all potatoes have a better flavour for being boiled in their skins, and peeled afterwards—something that will save us burning the ends of our fingers if, like me, they haven't got long fingernails. (The same sort of implement is needed for peeling freshly boiled beetroot.)

Further requirements include a foolproof gauge to tell you when all meat, corn on the cob, globe artichokes and asparagus are done; some way of storing saucepans that is not hideous to look at like those pyramidal stands, or involves the physical strain and deafening din of trying to get at the bottom saucepan of a nested pile on the shelf of a cupboard.

The final item is already invented. It is one of those simple and superbly practical cheese graters from Italy, which are shaped like a drum. You put it between your knees, grate the cheese on the lid and the cheese falls into the drum below. I've never yet seen one in this country, but arrange to bring one back from Italy next time, or get somebody to do it for you.

If you feel that to be able to grate cheese as easily as that is somehow cheating, forget it. You will not lose—in fact, you will consolidate—your status as a Coarse Cook, by cooking like an Italian peasant.

EXCUSES AND EXPLANATIONS

Qui s'excuse, s'accuse
FRENCH POLICE MOTTO

In Coarse Cookery no Excuses or Explanations are made post mortem, as they are in Coarse Bridge—or if they are, then only at the Coroner's Inquest where a lot of excusing and explaining may well prove necessary, if not unexpected.

Mistakes, gaffes, disasters, near-misses and direct mishits are excused, explained (and apologised for) as soon as they are laid on the table. Indeed, if possible, before that. Coarse Cooks have sympathetic friends (and God knows they need them) who appreciate honesty above all things—honesty, that is, in frankly admitting mistakes or failures. Whether the reasons put forward to excuse and explain these mistakes are strictly honest is another matter.

The most important and popular of these is without doubt the **Unexpected Telephone Call.**

This always occurs when the cook has just reached the most crucial point in her performance. It accounts for

Unbasted joints
Vegetables boiled to pulp
Curdled soup (you had just that moment put the egg-yolk in to thicken it)

Next in importance and popularity is the Act of God known as sudden **Low Gas Pressure**. (If you cook by electricity it is unwise to say there was a power-cut. It can be too easily checked.) Low Gas Pressure can be held responsible for

Undercooked joints
Inedible vegetables
Unsliceable, because still soft, hard-boiled eggs

The excuse of the **Unlooked-at Watch** covers all the above contingencies. You didn't look at your watch when you should have put the joint in the oven, the potatoes to cook, and so were late starting dinner. You didn't look at your watch when you should have taken the joint out of the oven, the potatoes off the gas, and so were late 'finalising' the dinner.

Unexpected Telephone Calls and Low Gas Pressures are excuses to be used sparingly, of course. Used too often they can give rise to suspicions that you are pushing your bad luck too far; while constant failure to look at your watch will eventually make your guests think your heart is not in Coarse Cookery. After all, its sole purpose is to cook to eat, and if you can't produce something worth eating you had better pack up.

There remain two points to be noted about the kind of near-catastrophe discussed so far. They are the attitude the cook is to adopt when (a) a dish is ruined by the late arrival of guests, and (b) when it is ruined by the dilatory and flustered cook himself.

In both cases the cook generously takes the blame, for the situation is not his fault in one case, but most certainly is in the second. In the first, he apologises for having started cooking too soon, in the second for having started too late.

The more trivial, everyday mistakes of under-seasoning, over-seasoning, under-flavouring and over-flavouring can be more or less brushed aside with a few well-tried bromides:

Too much garlic: 'Never mind, it's good for rheumatism.'

Too little salt: 'Well, you can always add, but you can't subtract.'

Too much salt: 'I thought sea-salt was supposed to be milder than ordinary salt.'

Too much black pepper: 'It must be the new lot from Fortnum's. I know I didn't use any more than usual.'

The foreign dish that hasn't come off: 'That's odd. I made it *exactly* as they do in Naples—except for the mozzarella cheese, of course.'

Too much garlic: 'Do you mean a bulb isn't the same thing as a clove?'

FIRST AID—*they say*

There are said to be several ways of dealing with mayonnaise that curdles. My own preference is for one which has a certain adventurousness about it.

You put an egg-yolk into a clean bowl and beat the curdled sauce into it, spoonful by spoonful. If, as is almost inevitable, you add the sauce too quickly it will curdle again. In which case, put another egg-yolk in another clean bowl and repeat the process.

Over-anxiety and impatience are likely to curdle this lot, too; and the next; and the next after that. When the sauce is finally ready and uncurdled you may well find that it contains anything up to four egg-yolks.

It is now so eggy that the only thing to do is to take a

tablespoonful of it, fry it, and see what sort of omelette it turns into.

A Crafty Hint

To keep down the smell of boiling brussels sprouts, cauliflower or cabbage in the kitchen, they say you should add a slice of lemon or a bit of lemon peel to the saucepan. Care must be exercised in this, however. Too much lemon can result in an unusual Corsican dish called *citron aux choux de Bruxelles*. It goes well with veal or fried fish.

NaCl Overspill (*too much salt again*)

If you are still confused about how much salt to use and have used too much of it in the soup, they say that if you put a couple of potatoes into the soup and boil them until they are cooked, they will absorb the salt.

WASHING UP

This is governed by strict rules of procedure and differentials, as laid down by S O S O (Society of Sink Operators). While the demarcation of who-does-what-next at the kitchen sink is not so inflexible as in some trade unions, and the division of labour in most of the various processes of stacking, washing, rinsing and drying is permitted, it is strictly forbidden for any husband to wash up saucepans, frying pans, baking tins or other receptacles used directly in the performance of actual cookery, and applies particularly to equipment used in cooking a Wiener Schnitzel.

This regulation has its origins in antiquity, or if it hasn't, its validity and sacrosanctity are nevertheless not to be disputed. Whether these utensils are washed up overnight, or left for Elsie la Journalière (*née* Mopp) to do in the morning, is a matter of no concern to the man of the house.

There must be a limit somewhere to the equality of the sexes.

5

Last Course

There are times, heaven knows, when most of us decide, to the tune of Irving Berlin's popular cantata, that 'There's No Cooking Like No Cooking'.

These are moments of natural depression which usually pass. But if they linger longer than is healthy, it is not a visit to the psychiatrist or the pub that is needed, but a few minutes of concentrated reflection on the Future of Food, Technology and the Tummy.

Sending men to the moon, as we know, not only created the non-stick frying pan, but also the possibility of a world eventually condemned by one social disaster or another to eat the sort of food eaten by astronauts. This consists of a huge variety of dehydrated morsels, ranging from meat cubes to apple pie, which are instantly rehydrated by a special water-pistol.

If the idea of this is too nauseating to contemplate, think of America's plans to build central food factories capable of producing 25 million frozen dinners a week—whole menus of meat, fish, veg, puds, soups, salads and sauces that can be reheated and served in a matter of minutes.

Meat and fish, did they say? Dr Mervyn Pyke, who reports gloomily on such things, tells us that there are factories already under construction in the United States where soya beans, peanuts, cottonseed, or half a dozen other sources of inexpensive proteins are processed to come out as bacon, beef, veal, chicken, venison or turkey at will. The end products are known as 'analogues', and a 'turkey-analogue' of soya-bean meal will be indistinguishable from the real thing.

Remembering that these technological miracles are being performed in the U.S.A., this is hardly surprising. To most Europeans, American meat has always tasted as though it was a synthesis of soya beans, peanuts, cottonseed or foam rubber.

The really appalling thought, which scarcely bears thinking, is the prospect that one day a broiler chicken will be as rare and twice as expensive as caviar.

Meanwhile, let all Coarse Cooks be comforted, first by the words of Athenaeus, who said, 'He who rightly cares for his own eating will not be a bad cook', and finally inspired by the reassurance of Brillat-Savarin, who so wisely reminded us that 'Mutual Appreciation of good food has a more marked influence on happiness than anything else in married life'.

Ringmer,
Sussex

BIBLIOGRAPHY

Below are listed some of the works which will help the reader to develop his Art and extend his knowledge of the historical background, philosophy and social significance of Coarse Cookery.

La vie horrifique du Grand Gargantua by François Rabelais
Aids to Scouting by Lord Baden-Powell
The Art of Coarse Cricket by Spike Hughes
The Art of Coarse Travel by Spike Hughes
The Art of Coarse Gardening by Spike Hughes
The Art of Coarse Bridge by Spike Hughes

FOR MORE ADVANCED READERS

Cold Dishes for All Seasons by Spike and Charmian Hughes

CONVERSION TABLES OF WEIGHTS AND MEASURES

Although it is highly improbable that any Coarse Cook
worth his salt and freshly ground black pepper will ever
weigh or measure anything in his kitchen, anyway, I have
thought it might be useful for him to know the exact
equivalents in metric terms (and *vice versa*) of the weights
and measures he won't be using.

1 Imperial gallon	=4·54346 litre
1 Republican (U.S.) gallon	=0·833 Imperial galls
1 Imperial pint	=0·56793 litre
1 Republican (or Democrat) pint	=0·4545968 litre
1 litre	=1·76077 pints
1 gill	=0·14198 litre
1 lb	=0·4535927 kilogram
	=(453·5927 grams)
1 gram	=0·564383 dram
1 kilogram	=15432·3487 grains
100 grams	=3 oz 8·4383 drams
¼ lb	=0·1133981 kilogram
1 decilitre	=0·176077 pint

The Coarse Cook may also be interested to know that:

7·29 in.	=1 link
300 yards of linen yarn	=1 cut
16 hands	=1 bundle
A peck loaf	=17 lb 6 oz 2 drams
8 lb of cheese	=1 clove
21 tons 4 cwt of coal	=1 barge or keel
2 stone of wool	=1 tod
1 puncheon of Scotch whisky	=112 to 120 gallons
600 herrings	=1 mease
615 herrings	=1 maze
40 lb of flour	=1 boll
4 fish	=1 warp
1 millilitre	=0·00176077 pint
5 millilitres	=1 National Health Service teaspoon

E. & O. E.